MW00774741

The Prime of My Days

The Prime of My Days

Lessons in the Prime of Life
from the Book of Job

MARK McCONNELL
Foreword by Steve Stroup

RESOURCE *Publications* · Eugene, Oregon

THE PRIME OF MY DAYS
Lessons in the Prime of Life from the Book of Job

Unless otherwise noted, Scripture quotations are from the New American Standard Bible, copyright 2002 by Zondervan.

Scripture quotations marked (NIV) are from the NIV Study Bible, copyright 1995 by Zondervan.

Scripture quotations marked (ESV) are from the ESV Bible (The Holy Bible, English Standard Version), copyright 2001 by Crossway.

Excerpt(s) from *The Four Loves* by C.S. Lewis reprinted by permission.

Excerpt(s) from "The Surprising Source of Joy: A Biblical Foundation for Christ-Centered Suffering" in *Reformed Faith & Practice* by Dr. Peter Lee reprinted by permission.

Excerpt(s) from "What If Honor Is Lost Altogether" in *TableTalk* by Dr. Albert Mohler reprinted by permission.

Excerpt(s) from *Your Days Are Numbered: A Closer Look At How We Spend Our Time & The Eternity Before Us* by John Perritt reprinted by permission.

Resource Publications
An Imprint of Wipf and Stock Publishers
199 W. 8th Ave., Suite 3
Eugene, OR 97401

www.wipfandstock.com

PAPERBACK ISBN: 978-1-7252-5954-6
HARDCOVER ISBN: 978-1-7252-5953-9
EBOOK ISBN: 978-1-7252-5955-3

Manufactured in the U.S.A.   03/18/20

To my wife,
Thank you for being my Editor-in-Chief and my favorite
trophy of God's grace. The blessing I prayed over you on the
day we wed is one I'm privileged to repeat today:

May God's hand be on your heart
May his word be on your mind
May his Spirit strengthen your soul
And may I never cease to love you well.

To my sons,
The pages that follow represent the best I could do with the
time, energy, and talent I could summon in my thirty-eighth
year. I hope you can glean some wisdom from my words. But
a day will come when your earthly father's wisdom will not be
sufficient to guide you. On that day, I pray that you will turn
to your Heavenly Father and use the tools you've been given to
mine his word for the inexhaustible riches to be found there.

Contents

Foreword

I first met Mark McConnell while serving in my former role as Senior Pastor at Federated Fellowship Church. During the latter part of my tenure, Mark and his family became members of our congregation. As time passed, I got to know Mark, his wife, Heather, and their two boys. Early on I noticed that Mark was a man of prayer who would consistently show up on Mondays at noon to pray with a group from our church body. Eventually, I approached Mark and asked if he would be interested in starting a group on Wednesday evenings to share group devotions and lift up the needs of our congregation, our community, and our missionaries around the world in prayer. That first Wednesday night there were only two attendees, Mark and myself. But over time our group outgrew the spare office where we first began meeting and bore witness to the formation of other prayer groups within our congregation; meeting at various times throughout the week. During those years of prayer, I learned more about Mark as a person and I was very impressed with him. He is a man's man. He works hard. He takes care of his family. He is a student of the word and loves to pray. My only concern when it comes to Mark is his insistence on rooting for the Boston Red Sox.

When Mark told me that he wrote a book on the twenty-ninth chapter of Job my first thought was, "This would be a good man to write this because I know his heart and the struggles he's faced in his life." My second thought was that Job is a book of the Bible of which preachers tend to steer clear. In my twenty years of ministry, I cannot begin to count how many times I have been asked what the book of Job is about and how one explains what happened to

Job. When I read *The Prime of My Days,* I was pleasantly surprised. Mark begins by giving us the background of the book, telling us where and how Job lived without getting lost in the weeds or going down rabbit trails, eventually leading us to the day Job lost everything. Mark then takes us to chapter twenty-nine, which is the very heart of Job and gives us the recipe for living life in its prime. Mark does not dodge the tough theological issues that come up in the book of Job. He hits them head-on, and while doing so, weaves in stories, history, sports, authoritative quotes, and glimpses of where Job points us to the New Testament.

The Prime of My Days is a fun read but also an insightful read if you want to get a handle on the book of Job and understand what living life in its prime is all about. I'm looking forward to Mark's next book!

STEVE STROUP
Associate Pastor
Federated Fellowship Church

Prologue

Club Executive: I've never heard of half of these guys and the ones I do know are way past their prime.

Charlie: Most of these guys never had a prime.

—*MAJOR LEAGUE*

Major League has to be one of my favorite baseball movies (tip: stick with the PG-13 version). For those who aren't familiar with the story, let me summarize the plot for you. The Cleveland Indians have come under new ownership. The new owner is no fan of Cleveland and wants to move the beleaguered franchise to Miami. But there's a catch. The club has a lease with the city that only allows the team to relocate in the event that attendance falls below a certain threshold. The new owner seizes upon this loophole and makes plans to field a roster of players who are so bad that no one will show up to watch them play. To paraphrase from the script, the players are way past their prime . . . if they ever had one.

For major league baseball players, the prime of their careers are fleeting windows of time when they are at the peak of their physical powers. Their ability to hit, throw, run, field, and catch are at their zenith. For most, it's a five to ten-year period stretching from their early twenties to their early thirties. A rare few players defy father time for a couple of extra years, but eventually the decline in their abilities relegates them to a diminished role on the team, and eventually, retirement.

The same is true for the rest of us. While our prime may not be dictated by our physical talents, inevitably a time will come when we look back on our lives and yearn for a season when we felt we were living life at its best. Others may grieve a life that never seemed to hit its stride. Like a promising young minor leaguer who suffers a career ending injury, circumstances have denied them a chance to reach their full potential. Observations like these beg the following questions:

- What does the "prime of my days" look like?
- Why do some people never experience it?
- Are there things I can do to ensure I'm living life in its prime?
- I feel like I'm past my prime. Can it be resurrected?
- Life's been long and hard. Is there any hope for me before the grave?

These are difficult questions. And only those who are very young, or who have lived the most charmed of lives escape asking them. For the vast majority of us there will come a day when we find these questions unavoidable.

THE NO GOOD, VERY BAD DAY

It was a cold and blustery day in February of 2016. Snow was still on the ground. In the Upper Midwest, February is sometimes described as January . . . reloaded. That day was classic February. I had only been at work an hour or so when I got a call from my wife. She was having seizures. She had been diagnosed with epilepsy a few months into our marriage and had been battling simple-partial seizures for nearly eight years. Medication had only proven marginally effective. Usually her seizures came in clusters, so I braced myself for a long day. My wife was a stay-at-home mom to our sons (ages one and four at the time) so typically I would've taken the rest of the day off, or depending on my schedule, worked from home to help keep an eye on them. But that day wasn't typical.

In June of the previous year, my wife's father had been diagnosed with stage-four lung cancer. In addition to raising an infant and a toddler, we found ourselves serving as the primary caregivers for a terminally ill cancer patient who lived an hour away. That day in February he was scheduled for radiation treatment. His health had deteriorated to the point where he could no longer drive himself to his appointments, and my wife was slated to chauffeur him that day. Obviously, she was in no condition to drive given her seizures. So, with assurances from my wife that she would check in often via text message, I hurriedly filed my PTO request at work and began the uneasy drive to the suburbs of Des Moines to pick up my father-in-law.

Upon pulling into his driveway, I hopped out of my truck and gave a courtesy knock at the side door. I heard his muffled voice from behind the door and I stepped inside to find him lying on the couch. He didn't look good. A stout man when healthy, he had lost a considerable amount of weight in the nine months since his diagnosis. The first time I met him, I remember shaking a hand that bore the size and shape of a bear claw attached to the forearm of Popeye the sailor. That same hand and forearm felt much smaller as I helped him into my truck for the drive downtown to Mercy Hospital's oncology treatment center.

He perked up a little as we drove to the appointment and settled into our chairs in the waiting room. My father-in-law was a talker, especially when he had a listener, and I provided a captive audience. We shared a love of the outdoors and I was genuinely interested in his past, so I was happy to oblige. Eventually his name was called, and I settled into a magazine as he made his way back for treatment. When he emerged thirty minutes later, he looked even worse than he did when I had picked him up.

We took advantage of a wheelchair as we made our way back to the parking ramp where I gingerly loaded him back into my pickup. Driving him home, we made a small detour to pick up a prescription for anti-nausea medication that was supposed to help with the side effects of the radiation. After a brief stop at the pharmacy drive-thru window, my pale father-in-law looked over at me and asked, "Do you have a weak stomach?" Confused, I blurted out a brief "no" before I realized he was giving me fair warning. In what has to be one of the cruelest ironies, he got sick in the passenger seat of my truck as his freshly compounded anti-nausea meds sat next to him. I was able to get him the rest of the way back to his place without further incident, and after getting him settled, I began the hour-long trek back home.

A lot of thoughts crossed my mind on that drive. To say the least, it had been a pretty tough day. I tried preaching to myself that tough days are to be expected. After all, Jesus warned us that "in this world you will have trouble."[1] But in my case, it seemed like the bad days had been outnumbering the good days for quite some time. What made it even harder to bear was that I was admittedly very tired and lonely. Our one-year-old had only successfully slept through the night once in his first year of life. My wife and I were utterly exhausted and would've been cast perfectly for a zombie film. And there was seemingly no cavalry coming to the rescue. We had re-located to a new town for a new job and in the hopes of finding new community a couple of years prior. I'd never had much trouble making friends up to that point in my life and figured this next chapter would be much of the same. But I'd had zero success at doing so thus far and was starting to lose hope that I ever would. It was against the backdrop of this internal debrief that I asked myself three simple questions:

1. What happened to the "good old days"?
2. Were they ever coming back?
3. What did the Bible have to say about situations like this?

Have you ever asked yourself these questions? Do you find yourself in a season of life where the bad days are far outnumbering the good? Do you find yourself yearning for a time when the pleasure of life was found in the simple act of living? Are you starting to lose hope that you will ever experience that again? If so, this book is for you.

1. John 16:33, NIV.

Ripefulness

Oh that I were as in months gone by . . .
As I was in the prime of my days . . .

—JOB 29:2-4A

I love autumn. I declare it the undisputed heavyweight champ among the four seasons. I love everything about it. I love the changing colors, when green leaves give way to vibrant hues of brown, yellow, orange, and red. I love it when suffocating heat and humidity give way to cool, crisp mornings and blue bird afternoons. I revel in the rare weather that affords comfort in shorts and a sweater, or jeans and a t-shirt. When the breezes are warm enough for light layers, but cool enough to be refreshing. I love watching the busyness of squirrels frantically storing up nuts for the long winter ahead. I love catching a glimpse of a buck deer at twilight, when the day's final rays of sunshine illuminate a set of antlers he's been growing all summer. I love the iridescent spots of a brook trout that get accentuated by fire-orange bellies as they prepare to spawn. I love football tailgates, bonfires, and the texture of a perfectly roasted marshmallow.

As a kid who grew up in the heart of the Heartland, I was keenly aware from a young age that autumn represents a season of abundance. It was not uncommon to experience traffic jams caused by combines, or see tractors staged in the high school parking lot for work in the fields after school. Dust from freshly picked acres would fill the air and intensify the effects of allergies and sunsets. Semi-trucks, towing trailers filled with grain, would operate around the clock as they transported the year's crop to grain bins, drying facilities, or barges waiting on the Mississippi. All of this activity served as a constant reminder that autumn was a time to take stock of and enjoy the fruit of one's labors.

In the twenty-ninth chapter of Job, we find a man nostalgic for his own season of abundance. In the first four verses of this incredible passage Job is yearning for the return of his prime:

> And Job again took up his discourse and said,
> "Oh that I were as in months gone by,
> As in the days when God watched over me;
> When his lamp shone over my head,
> And by His light I walked through darkness;
> As I was in *the prime of my days*,
> When the friendship of God was over my tent."[1]

A translation note in the New American Standard Bible renders the phrase "the *prime* of my days" more literally as "the days of my *autumn*." And the American Standard Version translates the original Hebrew as "the *ripeness* of my days."[2] I love the images these translations evoke. Consider a perfectly ripe apple waiting to be picked on a dewy morning. The morning sun glistens off the apple's shiny red skin. A single bite yields a satisfying crunch followed by a sweet juiciness that's hard to beat. It's a delight to the senses that's experienced best in the heart of autumn; after the orchardist has spent the year pruning, fertilizing, and protecting his trees from pests.

After a lifetime spent pruning, fertilizing, and protecting his relationships with God, his family, and his community, Job's life was like a perfectly ripe apple. Shiny to behold, satisfying to take part in, and sweetly savored. But almost overnight, he had it all taken away. The chilling frost of winter came without warning, and Job found himself pining for the good old days. You will be hard pressed to find a more startling or abrupt turn of events for a single character

1. Job 29:1–4, emphasis mine.
2. I guess neither American Standard version likes to be called "old."

6

anywhere in Scripture. But these events, Job's ensuing discourse, and the lessons we are to glean from them are better understood if we take some time to acquaint ourselves with our protagonist.

GETTING TO KNOW JOB

Scripture introduces us to Job in the first five verses of the book named for him:

> There was a man in the land of Uz whose name was Job; and that man was blameless, upright, fearing God and turning away from evil. Seven sons and three daughters were born to him. His possessions also were 7000 sheep, 3000 camels, 500 yoke of oxen, 500 female donkeys, and very many servants; and that man was the greatest of all the men of the east. His sons used to go and hold a feast in the house of each one on his day, and they would send and invite their three sisters to eat and drink with them. When the days of feasting had completed their cycle, Job would send and consecrate them, rising up early in the morning and offering burnt offerings according to the number of them all; for Job said, "Perhaps my sons have sinned and cursed God in their hearts." Thus Job did continually.[3]

What do these five verses tell us about Job? Quite a bit, if we're curious enough to ask a few background questions:

Where was Job from?

The first verse tells us immediately that Job was from the land of Uz. But this quickly begs a follow-up question. Where in the world is Uz?[4] The rest of the book provides limited clues, but if we do a little biblical sleuthing, we can get a rough fix on his position. Verse 3 tells us that Job "was the greatest of all the men of the east." But

3. Job 1:1–5.
4. Yep, I agree this question sounds like the beginning of a joke my seven-year-old would tell me.

east of where? If we take this to mean east of the Bible's geographical epicenter of Canaan (modern-day Israel), that still leaves us with a lot of earth to explore! But if we expand our search outside of the book of Job, we find a couple of helpful hints.

Uz is mentioned specifically only two other times in Scripture. The first is in Jeremiah 25:20, in a list of nations that will be judged by God. The nations listed immediately following Uz include Edom, Moab, and Ammon (located on the eastern edge of the Dead Sea), followed by the coastal regions of Tyre and Sidon (located on the Mediterranean). Assuming that Jeremiah was more or less listing these regions in geographical order from southeast to northwest, this would suggest a location somewhere southeast of the Dead Sea.[5] This theory gains support in Lamentations 4:21, where Jeremiah refers to an Edomite living in what we might assume would be the adjacent land of Uz.

What do we call the area immediately southeast of the Dead Sea? The southern half of modern-day Jordan. Why is this important? Well, as the old saying goes, the three most important things in business are "location, location, location." If Uz was where we think it was, then it would've placed Job's land holdings in or adjacent to the Fertile Crescent. This arc of land, stretching from the mouth of the Nile Delta in the southwest, up along the eastern coast of the Mediterranean, and eastward across the Tigris and Euphrates river basins was known as the agricultural breadbasket of the ancient world. This would explain the diversity of Job's livestock: oxen to plow the fertile ground near the Dead Sea, sheep to graze on the semi-arid land to the east, and camels for transportation across the Arabian desert. This region is also known as the "Cradle of Civilization" because several of the world's first urban centers were born out of it. Job would've lived at a key location along trading routes connecting these populated areas. In short, God placed him in an ideal location to prosper and build an influential reputation.

5. This might be a good time to break out that "Map of the Holy Land" in the back of your Bible or pull one up online. Don't worry, I'll wait.

What kind of man was Job?

The best kind. Verse 1 tells us he was "blameless, upright, fearing God, and turning away from evil." Job was a man of deep piety and unassailable integrity. If you lived in Uz, you'd want Job as your neighbor. If you were a kid, you'd want Job as your father. If you belonged to the servant class, you'd want Job as your master. If you had a daughter, you'd pray for a man like Job as a son-in-law.[6]

Did Job have a family?

Yes. A big one. He was married, and that union had produced ten children: seven sons and three daughters.[7] That's a lot of trips to whatever the equivalent of Costco was in ancient Uz. All of his children still lived near him and likely oversaw a portion of his immense holdings. The children were so close-knit that they created a sibling social calendar. Everyone would gather at one of the respective brother's homes for a party on a regular basis. All of the siblings were invited, including the three sisters. I guarantee that any parent reading this just whispered a silent prayer along the lines of, "Dear God, please help my children get along this well." This must've been an enormous source of pride and joy for Job.

How old was Job?

The text doesn't tell us. But we can make an educated guess. Let's revisit our key phrase from Job 29:4. In referring to the "days of my autumn," Job was likely offering us a clue to his age in addition to the quality of life he was living. After all, authors have been using the four seasons as a literary device for denoting age forever. It's telling that Job didn't refer to himself as a "spring chicken," one of the "boys of summer," or as "old man winter." The ages of Job's children also offer us a clue. We don't know their precise ages or the

6. "I have made a covenant with my eyes not to look lustfully at a young woman" (Job 31:1, NIV).

7. See Job 2:9.

order of their birth, but we do know that each of the seven brothers lived in his own home. This indicates that at the very least, seven of Job's ten children were adults. Even if Job had become a father at a fairly young age, it's safe to assume that at this point in his life he was firmly into what we'd consider today to be middle age, probably later middle age.

Was Job lower class, middle class, or upper class?

Job was what we'd refer to today as a "one percenter." He was uber-wealthy. Verse 3 enumerates his possessions to include:

- Seven thousand sheep
- Three thousand camels
- Five hundred yoke of oxen (There are two oxen in a yoke. You can do the math.)
- Five hundred female donkeys (I'm guessing he had a few males too.)
- Very many servants

These are staggering numbers, even by today's standards. But in ancient times, when there was no such thing as a gold standard, net worth, or market valuation; livestock was the primary method of assessing one's wealth. These numbers would've been almost unfathomable to his contemporaries. If Warren Buffet is the "Oracle of Omaha," Job was the "Utterer of Uz."

When did Job live?

This is probably the most difficult of our background questions to answer. The book of Job mentions no specific calendar date or historical reference that would offer much in the way of clues. As such, determining an exact date, or even a fairly broad window of time as to when the events of the book took place is a problem. However, there are enough salient details in chapter 1 to place Job in or around a specific biblical era.

As we just mentioned, Job's immense wealth was indicated by the numbers of his livestock and servants. This points to a fairly early date as later biblical accounts indicate wealth in terms of precious metals,[8] gems,[9] or monetary units,[10] which were part of fully formed currencies. Verse 5 mentions that Job offered sacrifices on behalf of his family. This practice would have been discontinued after the establishment of the priesthood in Exodus. So, we can safely place Job before Moses on the historical timeline.

If we skip to much later in the book,[11] we find that Job lived 140 years *after* the events described therein. This would indicate that Job lived to an age of somewhere in the neighborhood of two hundred years old. If we note the gradual decline in lifespan of biblical characters after the flood, we see that no one lived past the age of two hundred after Terah, the father of Abraham. It's at this point that we can say with a fair amount of confidence that Job lived during the patriarchal period after Noah, but before Abraham. Though he was probably closer to being a contemporary of the latter.

HAVE YOU CONSIDERED MY SERVANT JOB?

Now that we know a little more about Job's circumstances, let's take a moment to examine the narrative that serves as the backdrop to our main text. Remember, Job had it all. By his own telling he was a man in his prime. How did it all unravel for him? Let's pick up where we left off in chapter 1:

> Now there was a day when the sons of God came to present themselves before the Lord, and Satan also came among them. The Lord said to Satan, "From where do you come?" Then Satan answered the Lord and said, "From roaming about on the earth and walking around on it." The Lord said to Satan, "Have you considered My servant Job? For there is no one like him on the earth, a blameless

8. Gen 13:2.
9. Exod 28.
10. Matt 20:2.
11. Job 42:16.

and upright man, fearing God and turning away from evil." Then Satan answered the Lord, "Does Job fear God for nothing? Have You not made a hedge about him and his house and all that he has, on every side? You have blessed the work of his hands, and his possessions have increased in the land. But put forth Your hand now and touch all that he has; he will surely curse You to Your face." Then the Lord said to Satan, "Behold, all that he has is in your power, only do not put forth your hand on him." So Satan departed from the presence of the Lord.[12]

This is one of the few places in Scripture where we are afforded a peek behind the curtain, so to speak, and granted a glimpse of the divine counsel. The Lord is holding court with his angels when the fallen one makes an appearance. Satan cannot stand to see God glorified so he has spent his time prowling[13] over the face of the earth, looking for an opportunity to attack God's image bearers. In an affront to Satan, God holds up Job as an example of holiness. Of all of God's children, Satan has had the least luck with Job. Despite his best attempts to date, Job remains "blameless and upright . . . fearing God and turning away from evil." Always the accuser,[14] Satan asserts that Job's faith has been cheaply bought. Job has lived a charmed life. He's found an ace in every hand he's ever been dealt. If God were to remove his protection, surely the frame of his faith would fold like a tent in a windstorm. God sees Satan's tactic for what it is, a desperate attempt to open a gap. A gap just wide enough to forever drive a wedge between God and one of his anointed ones. To prove the sincerity of Job's faith he allows Satan to test Job, but with one caveat. Satan cannot lay a hand against Job's person. The enemy wastes no time in doing his worst:

Now on the day when his sons and daughters were eating and drinking wine in their oldest brother's house, a messenger came to Job and said, "The oxen were plowing and the donkeys feeding beside them, and the Sabeans attacked and took them. They also slew the servants with

12. Job 1:6–12.
13. 1 Pet 5:8.
14. Rev 12:10.

the edge of the sword, and I alone have escaped to tell you." While he was still speaking, another also came and said, "The fire of God fell from heaven and burned up the sheep and the servants and consumed them, and I alone have escaped to tell you." While he was still speaking, another also came and said, "The Chaldeans formed three bands and made a raid on the camels and took them and slew the servants with the edge of the sword, and I alone have escaped to tell you." While he was still speaking, another also came and said, "Your sons and your daughters were eating and drinking wine in their oldest brother's house, and behold, a great wind came from across the wilderness and struck the four corners of the house, and it fell on the young people and they died, and I alone have escaped to tell you." Then Job arose and tore his robe and shaved his head, and he fell to the ground and worshiped. He said, "Naked I came from my mother's womb, and naked I shall return there. The Lord gave and the Lord has taken away. Blessed be the name of the Lord." Through all this Job did not sin nor did he blame God.[15]

In ten short verses, a matter of minutes for Job, the greatest man of the East was reduced to the least. All of his wealth was stolen, his servants murdered, and his children killed in a natural disaster. The evil one, whose *modus operandi* is to "steal and kill and destroy,"[16] had done just that. The blissful "days of autumn" that Job had been enjoying were lost, not to a gentle frost, but to a fierce blizzard. I doubt that most people reading this can fathom this much loss in this short a period of time. I certainly can't. Any attempt to process it would crush the most mentally strong among us. But the most amazing thing happens. Job does not do what we would expect someone in this situation to do. He doesn't take his own life to escape the dark abyss of his grief. He doesn't lose grip of his sanity. He doesn't set out to take revenge on those who have stolen from him. He doesn't abandon his faith. Instead, he does four extraordinary things:

15. Job 1:13–22.
16. John 10:10.

1. He speaks truth to himself and those around him. (The Lord gave and the Lord has taken away.)

2. He blesses the name of the Lord.

3. He refuses to medicate his pain with sin.

4. He refuses to blame God.

It's not exactly the outcome Satan was hoping for. Unfortunately for Job, the enemy is never easily deterred:

> Again there was a day when the sons of God came to present themselves before the Lord, and Satan also came among them to present himself before the Lord. The Lord said to Satan, "Where have you come from?" Then Satan answered the Lord and said, "From roaming about on the earth and walking around on it." The Lord said to Satan, "Have you considered My servant Job? For there is no one like him on the earth, a blameless and upright man fearing God and turning away from evil. And he still holds fast his integrity, although you incited Me against him to ruin without cause." Satan answered the Lord and said, "Skin for skin! Yes, all that a man has he will give for his life. However, put forth Your hand now, and touch his bone and his flesh; he will curse You to Your face." So the Lord said to Satan, "Behold, he is in your power, only spare his life." Then Satan went out from the presence of the Lord and smote Job with sore boils from the sole of this foot to the crown of his head. And he took a potsherd to scrape himself while he was sitting among the ashes. Then his wife said to him, "Do you still hold fast your integrity? Curse God and die!" But he said to her, "You speak as one of the foolish women speaks. Shall we indeed accept good from God and not accept adversity?" In all this Job did not sin with his lips.[17]

Once again, we find ourselves witness to the divine counsel. The account starts much the same as the first counsel, but God knows what Satan has been up to. And Satan knows that he knows. And for Satan, it's infuriating. His plans have been thwarted. He is

17. Job 2:1–10.

incensed when God victoriously repeats his question from their first exchange, "Have you considered My servant Job? . . . he *still* holds fast his integrity . . ." Satan is now desperate. The gap he was hoping to exploit wasn't wide enough for his wedge, so he does what he's done since the fall. He tries a different angle. He lobbies for the rules to be changed. He contends that God didn't give him a fair shake in the first round. God may have won the battle, but if God will let him hit Job where it really hurts, surely he will win the war. Confident in Job's fidelity, God relents. He removes the restriction on Job's person. The only thing Satan must spare is his life. Satan eagerly goes to work and afflicts Job with painful boils over his entire body.

Why boils? Scripture doesn't say. But if you'll allow me a moment of sanctified imagination, I'll venture a guess. Our skin is the largest organ in our body. It's how we feel the world around us. It's what everyone sees. When we struggle with acne, we feel embarrassed by our appearance. When we stumble into poison ivy, the resulting itch is maddening. When we have an open sore, we worry about infection. Our skin is the tent covering that shields us from the rainstorms of life. If Satan wanted to inflict someone in a way that would convince them, beyond the shadow of a doubt, that God had removed his protection for good, full body boils would be a pretty sinister way to go.

The effect on Job is horrifying. It was too much for his wife. Remember, she too had lost everything. Her wealth, her servants, and her children were all gone. The one love she has left has been stricken so severely that she can scarcely look at him. In a moment of hysteria, she implores her husband to beg God for death. Job's only consolation is a broken piece of pottery, used to pick the scabs off his blistering body. Surely this would be enough to push Job over the edge. How could this not rock his faith in God to the core? If ever there were justification to seek solace in things of this world, this would be it. But Job is steadfast in his response to the calamity that has struck him:

1. He speaks truth to himself and to his wife. (Shall we indeed accept good from God and not accept adversity?)
2. He refuses to medicate his pain with sin.

It's a response like this that commands our attention and demands we take notice as the rest of Job's story unfolds. It's in the midst of these devastating circumstances that we fast forward to the twenty-ninth chapter of the book:

> Oh that I were as in months gone by . . . As I was in the
> prime of my days . . .

Why is it important to study one man's wistful recollection of his prime? In a book that through the ages has served as arguably the preeminent text on human suffering; why focus on the one chapter dedicated to Job's "good old days"? There are three good reasons I can think of:

Job proffers us wisdom

When I studied Job in seminary it was included within a larger course in the biblical studies curriculum that was simply named "Poets." Along with Psalms, Proverbs, Ecclesiastes, Song of Solomon, and Lamentations, Job rounds out the canon of poetry in Old Testament Scripture. Indeed, the bulk of the book is comprised of dialogue between Job and his friends set in poetic form. But if we merely classify Job as a book of poetry sandwiched between a prologue and epilogue of prose, we do Scripture, and ourselves, a great injustice. "According to The NIV Complete Concordance the word wisdom occurs in the book of Job twenty-three times. . . . in addition we find the word wise, usually in the nominal form 'the wise,' seven times."[18] These are thirty signposts telling us that Job is also a book of wisdom.

Job was a wise man to begin with. God never regards fools the way he regards Job in the divine counsel. But hindsight, as they say, is 20/20. In Job 29, we encounter a man who has exercised deep reflection. Few things make the truth clearer than time and hardship. Job had plenty of both. What we are privy to is the clarity of a man who had examined his past and had identified the things that had been lost which were of highest value. He enumerates for us those

18. van Selms, *Job: A Practical Commentary,* 13–14.

things which bring the greatest satisfaction in life. What Job offers us is wisdom. We would do well to listen.[19]

Job points us to Christ

Job is what theologians refer to as a "type" of Christ. What is a type? Put simply, it is an earthly shadow cast by a heavenly reality.[20] Types are found all over the pages of Scripture. Beyond that, one could argue that the natural world is full of types, all pointing us to the work of the cross. Types are incomplete copies that introduce us to a more fully formed design.

Let me see if I can explain using an example most of us can relate to. For many of us, our first experience driving a car is with the matchbox variety. These miniature copies bear a passing resemblance to an actual automobile. They look like a car, possess axles and wheels, and will move across a smooth surface when propelled by an outside force (in this case, our chubby little fingers). They serve as a fun introduction to the general look and feel of an actual car, but we learn pretty quickly that they are not what my four-year-old would call "the real deal." Later in childhood, if we're very lucky, we are taken to a go-kart track. Here we're given the opportunity to test drive a more fully formed type of car. The cars are larger than the matchbox variety, but still smaller than the genuine article. They are now self-propelled (via the lawn mower engine mounted on the back), include gas and brake pedals for operation, a wheel for steering, and seat belts for safety. They delightfully reveal to us much more about the true nature of an actual car, but still fall short of the real thing.

Like the matchbox car and go-kart, Scripture provides types that progressively reveal more about God's plan through the history of redemption. A good example from the Old Testament is the tabernacle, the official meeting place of God and his people as instituted in the pages of Exodus. We are given lots of details about what is necessary to obtain communion with God by reading about

19. Prov 3:13.
20. Heb 8:5.

the construction of the tabernacle. Still more details are revealed upon construction of the tabernacle's successor, the temple in Jerusalem, as laid out in 1 Chronicles and 2 Chronicles. But it is not until we encounter the true high priest, God's own Son, that the door is opened to the sanctuary of "the true tabernacle, which the Lord pitched, not man."[21]

Types are not limited to material objects referenced throughout the Old Testament narrative. Several of the actual characters of the Bible also serve as types. Salvation is not to be found in any of them, but certain aspects of their lives point us to our Savior. Job was one of these types. He points us to Christ in several ways. We will explore the typology of Job more in the chapters ahead, but let me give you an example as a baseline. When studios want to market a soon-to-be-released film, they will often release a trailer to be played during the "Coming Attractions" segment preceding a currently featured attraction. The trailer is meant to provide a glimpse of what one can expect from the setting, characters, and plot of the upcoming film. One way in which Job serves as a trailer for the coming attraction of Christ is by playing the part of a righteous servant who suffered undeservedly. Though not perfect by his own admission, Job's upright life and subsequent suffering provide us a sneak preview of the life and passion of Christ.[22]

Job provides us a recipe

Speaking of movies, in 1987 Hollywood released the film *The Secret of My Success*. In this romantic comedy the main character, Brantley Foster (played by Michael J. Fox), is a "wet behind the ears" college graduate from Kansas. He moves to New York City, determined to find success in the world of high finance. In a zany series of events, Brantley lands an entry-level job at his uncle's corporation, creates a fictitious identity and poses as a newly hired junior executive, falls in love with a fellow executive team member, and by exposing the ineptitude of his uncle's leadership, is minted the corporation's

21. Heb 8:2.
22. Job 42:6.

new leader. The film's plot highlights his meteoric rise from the first rung to the top rung of the corporate ladder in a matter of weeks and audiences loved it to the tune of $110 million at the box office.[23]

And why did movie goers love it so much? Because we are naturally infatuated with success. We're all in search of the secret that will unlock some of the best of what life has to offer. We want to reverse engineer the recipe for living life in its prime. But what if God has hidden the recipe in plain sight? Job's prime was more prime than our prime will ever be. And (spoiler alert) he had two of them! By any standard, worldly or godly, Job was the most successful man of his age. But more importantly, Job's prime was lived out in a way that was not only pleasing to him, but pleasing to God. By studying Job 29, we're issued a copy of the recipe for living life in its prime. A prime of life that is not only a delight to us, but more importantly, glorifying to God. But the ingredients listed in this recipe may just surprise you . . .

---

23. "The Secret of My Success."

God-Friend

...When the friendship of God was over my tent;
When the Almighty was yet with me ...

—JOB 29:4B–5A

In recent years I've developed an affinity for Cajun cuisine. I've never been to Louisiana, but I'm not sure I've met better comfort food than the likes of red beans and rice, jambalaya, or shrimp étouffée. I've even tried my hand at cooking a few of these dishes, albeit with mixed results. The only Cajun recipe I feel that I've mastered thus far is for gumbo. This soupy concoction is built upon the "holy trinity" of onions, celery, and bell peppers. Served with a dollop of white rice and a side of French bread, it's a welcome treat at the end of a long work week. Any cook familiar with gumbo will tell you the key to a good batch is in the roux. The roux is the base ingredient of the dish. It consists simply of flour and oil and is prepared by constantly stirring the mixture over a low-medium heat source. The idea is to slowly "cook" the flour in the oil until the mix turns a color best described as somewhere between peanut butter and chocolate. Heat too quickly or forget to stir for too long and the roux will burn, forcing you to start over. But if you get the roux right, the rest of the dish is almost guaranteed to turn out great.

In Job 29 we are told of a primary ingredient that is necessary for living life in its prime. But it's not what many would expect. In a BBC Future article published in 2015, the authors scoured medical research to identify ages at which factors contributing to one's prime of life peaked.[1] These included things you might expect such as when people reported having the highest levels of physical fitness, cognitive ability and memory, knowledge acquisition, sexual prowess, and overall satisfaction. Depending on who you talk to, other factors might also be considered. Seasons of greatest financial security, independence, freedom, or mobility might also contribute to one's prime. For others, the season when they had the biggest and/or closest social support network might indicate when life was at its best. But as Job recounts the elements of his prime, none of these things receive top billing. For Job, the roux in the recipe for prime living consisted of one key ingredient: the friendship of God.

MOST EXCELLENT THEOPHILUS

In the New Testament, the apostle Paul's companion, Luke, addresses both the Gospel bearing his name and the book of Acts to his friend, the "most excellent" Theophilus. We don't know much about Theophilus, other than he has one of the best names in the Bible. It's a construction of two Greek words: Theo, from the root *theos*, meaning "God"; and philus, from the root *philia*, meaning "Friend." His name, translated literally, is "God-friend," or as we might render it in modern English, "Friend of God." Even though Luke was addressing this first-century saint directly as he began these accounts, his salutation remains equally appropriate for any believer who begins reading these two books today. Why? Because in John's Gospel we are informed of an incredible truth about ourselves:

> No longer do I call you slaves, for the slave does not know what his master is doing; but I have called you *friends* . . .[2]

The Holy Spirit addresses the Gospel of Luke and the book of Acts to "God-friend" because that's who we are. The Creator of

1. Robson, "What's the Prime of Your Life?"
2. John 15:15a, emphasis mine.

the universe desires friendship with us. Not only does he desire it, but he reckons the relationship established by his Son's work on the cross. Christianity is unique in that an omnipotent, omniscient, omnipresent God wants us to find our satisfaction, not merely in serving him, but in knowing him. Even centuries prior to the revelation of Christ, Job understood this intimately. As he laments the loss of his prime, it's not his health or wealth he misses most; it's God's friendship. He mentions it first in the list of things he's lost because it was his greatest source of joy.

The Westminster Shorter Catechism begins by posing the question, "What is the chief end of man?" The answer supplied is: "Man's chief end is to glorify God, and to enjoy Him forever." The enjoyment of God is manifested in large part through our friendship with him. But it's exactly this friendship that most Christians struggle to embrace. Why? I think C. S. Lewis put it well when he said:

> Friendship is . . . the least natural of loves . . . without Eros [erotic love] none of us would have been begotten and without Affection none of us would have been reared; but we can live and breed without Friendship. The species, biologically considered, has no need of it. The pack or herd—the community—may even dislike and distrust it. Its leaders very often do.[3]

Our culture simply does not place a premium on friendship. Think about it. Much of our popular music places romantic love on a pedestal. You'll have no trouble finding articles or books extolling the virtues of parental affection (or bemoaning the lack thereof). But it's a little tougher locating books, movies, music, or web sites devoted primarily to the art of finding and keeping "buddies." And as Lewis suggests, oftentimes the world's attitude toward friendship oscillates somewhere between indifference and veiled hostility. Our careers provide a sobering example. According to Gallup research, only two in ten American workers strongly agree that they have a best friend at work.[4] The place where most adult Americans spend the majority of their waking hours is largely devoid of deep

3. Lewis, *The Four Loves*, 58.
4. *State of the American Workplace*, 118.

friendship. Sadly, too many workplace leaders view friendship among their subordinates as a "nice to have," a distraction, or in some cases, an outright threat. As a result, our workplaces are filled with lonely workers.

What makes matters worse is that when it comes to making friends, we seem to get worse with age. According to a study from Oxford University and the University of Finland, our number of friends reaches its peak at the age of twenty-five.[5] From there, and there's no way to sugar coat it, the number drops off a cliff. The reasons why could fill another book. But I think it's safe to say that somewhere in early adulthood we lose track of the fundamentals of friendship. This is tragic because it's through our horizontal relationships (friendship with each other) that we learn how to enjoy a vertical relationship (friendship with God). So, for those of us whose twenty-fifth birthday is in our rearview mirror (and you youngsters who could teach the rest of us a thing or two) let's devote a few pages to the framework of friendship.

THE BIRTH OF FRIENDSHIP

Ordained Encounter

It's important to realize that each of our friendships begin with a divine appointment. God carefully and intentionally orchestrates the unique circumstances necessary for friendships to be formed. Again, Lewis provides insight:

> But in Friendship . . . we think we have chosen our peers. In reality, a few years' difference in the dates of our births, a few more miles between certain houses, the choice of one university instead of another, posting to different regiments, the accident of a topic being raised or not raised at a first meeting—any of these chances might have kept us apart. But, for a Christian, there are, strictly speaking no chances. A secret Master of the Ceremonies has been at work. . . . The Friendship is not a reward for

5. Bhattacharya, "Sex differences."

our discrimination and good taste in finding one another out. It is the instrument by which God reveals to each the beauties of all the others.[6]

If you want a good exercise in meditating on providence (in this case, God's role in forming our friendships), begin by making a list of your closest friends. With these friends in mind, start taking a stroll down memory lane:

- When did you meet them?
- How did your paths cross?
- How old were you when you met?
- What was the context of your first interaction?
- What was the topic of your first discussion?
- Why was that top of mind for both of you in that moment?

Now, one by one, imagine the implications of changing even one of those details:

- What if you'd met them in high school instead of college?
- What if you'd never gone to that fraternity rush event?
- What if you'd been thirty instead of twenty?
- What if you'd met them in Bible study instead of a board meeting?
- What if the topic of that forum had been leadership principles instead of fly-fishing strategies?
- What if your mind had been on your calculus final instead of your broken heart?

Imagine how different your life would've been! If just one detail had been different, it's quite possible that those you call your dearest friends would've remained strangers forever. Imagine the tragedy of never having had the privilege of knowing them. Imagine what it would've been like to experience that season of life without their love, support, and camaraderie. Imagine not being able to look back with a joyful heart on memories that will always make you smile. This sort of reflective meditation often results in a quick series of emotions. It starts with a brief moment of panic as we shudder to

6. Lewis, *The Four Loves*, 89.

think what we might have missed. Our panic quickly gives way to relief as we refocus on reality; our friendships and our memories are thankfully intact. And our relief soon morphs into gratitude as we take stock of how we've been blessed. And we should be grateful. After all, the Great Matchmaker was responsible for all of it. It was by his will that all of our friendships got their start, including our friendship with him.

We are God's friends only because he initiated the relationship. Another peek at John's Gospel reveals this truth:

You did not choose Me but I chose you . . .[7]

Those who become God's friends owe their relationship to a conscious choice on the part of God. He wanted to be friends, so he ordained an encounter with him to get things started. This encounter may take countless forms. For some, it may be a thunderbolt from the pulpit that hits us squarely between eyes. For others, a tear-stained Bible bears evidence of a heart that has been pierced by God's word for the first time. Some may encounter him in a foxhole, others may find him in a bar. Some are introduced to God by pastors, family, or friends. Others are introduced by strangers. Some glimpse him on the mountaintop. Others blindly bump into him in the pit. The encounter is different for all of us, but the result is the same. God wanted to meet us, so he did.

Common Interest

As all of us can attest, merely crossing paths with someone does not mean you become friends with them. A first encounter may provide a spark, but something more is required to fan the flame of friendship. What is that something? A common interest. Friends need something they can share. Something that greases the skids of conversation. Something that's important to both of them. It may be something minor, like a shared fondness for a particular flavor of

---

7. John 15:16a.

ice cream.[8] Or it may be something major, like a mission to revitalize a neighborhood. Lewis summed it up nicely when he said:

> Friendship arises out of mere Companionship when two or more of the companions discover that they have in common some insight or interest or even taste which the others do not share and which, till that moment, each believed to be his own unique treasure (or burden). The typical expression of opening Friendship would be something like, "What? You too? I thought I was the only one."[9]

I think the moment of, "What? You Too?" is a powerful picture of our need to relate. It's a moment of immense hope and anticipation because we know that the discussion and activity that follows often serves as the cornerstone of friendship. The more important the common interest, the closer the potential friendship.

God can be and should be our closest friend because our common interest is of eternal consequence. When our ordained encounter with God comes to pass, the conversation inevitably unfolds along the lines Lewis suggests:

God: "So what's something you spend a lot of time thinking about these days?"

Us: "Honestly, I'm really preoccupied with the state of my soul."

God: "What? You too?"

We're interested in being saved. God is interested in doing the saving. Sounds like the basis of a beautiful friendship.

THE GROWTH OF FRIENDSHIP

Shared Revelation

We've covered how friendships are born. Now let's touch on how friendships grow. After an ordained encounter takes place and a

8. I highly recommend Bunny Tracks produced by the good people at Blue Bunny.

9. Lewis, *The Four Loves*, 65.

common interest is discovered, the depth of an ensuing friendship is determined in large part by how much of themselves both parties are willing to share with each other. Casual friends keep things light and near the surface. Their conversations may never get past the Red Sox' pitching woes. And that's OK. Not every friend can reside within your inner circle. But for a friendship to evolve from casual to close, the parties must begin to reveal more of themselves.

I think this is where the wheels start to come off for many of us. As children, this is easier. Our personal histories don't go back very far so there isn't as much for us to reveal. And odds are, many of our childhood friends experienced or observed many of the more notable events of our youth firsthand. Revelation isn't as important when you were an eyewitness. But as adults, we're not privy to the life-shaping events of those we meet. Intimacy doesn't take place until we work up the courage to share a piece of our past that informed who we are today. And it isn't easy to share unless the other party asks in a way that invites an authentic response.

Our friendship with God can only deepen to the extent we are willing to be real with him about what is on our mind and on our heart. Yet, many Christians hold something back. This is where our experience with earthly relationships can prove to be a hindrance. Most of us stop short of offering our whole selves in friendship for fear of getting hurt. We've been burned in the past, so why go back to the source of the heat? And even if we're confident we can trust the other party, sometimes we censor what we share because we don't think the other person can handle it. After all, life is messy and sometimes there aren't enough mops to go around. If that weren't enough, all of us have things we're not proud of. We'd just as soon ensure that the regrettable things in our past never see the light of day, let alone be shared in the counsel of our friends.

While these are understandable (and at times, wise) cautions to heed when approaching our earthly friendships, they aren't help-ful in deepening our friendship with God. Why? Because he knows it all anyway! King David knew this better than anyone when he wrote:

> O LORD, You have searched me and known me. You
> know when I sit down and when I rise up; You under-
> stand my thought from afar. You scrutinize my path and
> my lying down, And are intimately acquainted with all
> my ways. Even before there is a word on my tongue, Be-
> hold, O LORD, You know it all. You have enclosed me
> behind and before, And laid Your hand upon me. . . .
> Where can I go from Your Spirit? Or where can I flee
> from Your presence? If I ascend to heaven, You are there;
> If I make my bed in Sheol, behold, You are there. If I take
> the wings of the dawn, If I dwell in the remotest part of
> the sea, Even there Your hand will lead me, And Your
> right hand will lay hold of me . . . in Your book were all
> written The days that were ordained for me, When as yet
> there was not one of them.[10]

God considered David a "man after His own heart" which
sounds an awful lot like a "God-friend" to me.[11] The depth of
David's friendship with God can be traced directly to the amount
of his heart he was willing to reveal. The Psalms are littered with
examples showing that David rarely held anything back in his communion with God. Neither should we. We would do well to imitate
this aspect of his friendship with the Almighty.

Of course, true friendship requires that revelation be made by
both parties. Lopsided relationships in which one friend bares his
soul while the other reveals little are not healthy, and typically don't
last very long. Luckily, God does not fail to reveal his heart in his
friendship with us. He does so through his word. The Bible tells us
everything we need to know in order to enjoy an intimate relationship with God. It's in the pages of Scripture that God reveals to us
the details of his personality:

- He reveals what makes him angry.[12]
- He reveals what's grieved his heart.[13]

---

10. Ps 139:1–16.

11. 1 Sam 13:14.

12. Rom 1:18.

13. Gen 6:5–6.

- He reveals what he hates.[14]
- He reveals what makes him jealous.[15]
- He reveals what brings him joy.[16]
- He reveals who makes him laugh.[17]
- He reveals whom he loves.[18]

And the list goes on and on. . . . The perspicuity of the Bible ensures that our friendship with God will never be in danger of ending up like an old married couple who have run out of things to talk about. Whether we're reading the Bible for the first time or the fortieth time, God never fails to reveal himself in new ways. And he will do so eternally. God doesn't desire to be a mere acquaintance of ours. He desires to be our friend. And while this friend can never be fully understood, he can be known. God is never guilty of holding back a piece of his heart in his relationship with us. Or put in romantic terms, God doesn't play "hard to get." As my systematic theology professor, Dr. Douglas Kelly, used to say, "If you want God, you can have Him!"

Shared Communication

Any marriage counselor worth his or her salt will tell you that loving, consistent communication is essential to a healthy marriage. Most pre-marital counseling curriculums will devote at least one session to the topic. And a lack of quality communication has to make most counselors' list of top issues they deal with on a week-to-week basis. Simply put, shared communication is key to the health of any relationship.

Like most married men, I can relate to this foundational truth firsthand. As a natural introvert who works in a people-centric profession, my need (and desire) for communication is often running

14. Prov 6:16–19.
15. Exod 20:4–5.
16. Zeph 3:17.
17. Ps 37:13.
18. Prov 8:17.

on fumes by the end of the day. However, in his wisdom, God has seen fit to bless me with a natural extrovert for a wife. As a result, oftentimes I arrive home and am greeted by a bride whose need (and desire) for communication outpaces my own. Most days she lovingly attempts to provide me with a little breathing room (my kids, not so much) before diving headlong into marital discourse. But eventually, her inner extrovert wins out and she gently prods me, like she used to prod our boys when they were toddlers, to "use your words."

And it's important that I do. As my wife's best earthly friend, she needs to feel close to me. And she can't feel close to me unless I do my part to meet her conversational needs. The same is true for any friendship. We feel closer to the friends we consistently communicate with. We feel more distant from the friends we rarely converse with, even if they live next door. This becomes even more evident when the circumstances of life place distance between us and one of our friends, resulting in our drifting apart. But I would contend it's not the distance that causes us to drift, it's the lack of consistent communication that so often accompanies it.

This same sort of drift can adversely affect our friendship with God. For all of us, seasons will come when we may confess to others that we don't feel as close to God anymore. And while there may be a number of reasons for this, it's not because God has in any way moved away from us.[19] One of my first questions for anyone who says this would be, "When was the last time you talked to him?"

A close friendship with God requires consistent communication. And consistent communication with God comes in the form of prayer. Like a Wi-Fi signal in your favorite coffee shop, prayer is the medium by which we connect with God. Maintaining a friendship with God without prayer is like trying to surf the web with your Wi-Fi turned off. You won't get much data from either.

Few people in the annals of church history understood this better than Teresa of Avila. This sixteenth-century Carmelite nun considered prayer to be:

---

19. ". . . the Lord is near" (Phil 4:5b).

... nothing else than intimate sharing between friends; it means taking time frequently to be alone with him who we know loves us.[20]

In this short statement, Teresa reminds us that prayer is our pathway to intimate friendship with God. But intimacy requires effort. And Teresa spells out how we should focus this effort. A healthy prayer life requires that we (at a minimum):

- Carve out time for it.[21]
- Do so frequently.[22]
- Seek him in solitude.[23]
- Meditate on his love.[24]

Four simple tasks on paper. Four excruciating spiritual disciplines in practice. But the reward of doing so is an open line of communication with God. And friends who communicate openly feel a lot closer than those who don't.

Shared Suffering

We all have people in our lives who live by the mantra, "I'm not here for a long time; I'm here for a good time." They're the first to show up at a party on Friday night. They're the last to show up to help us move a couch early on Saturday morning. There's a term for these people. We call them "fair weather friends." We can still enjoy their company. But we're not likely to ask them to stand up with us at our wedding or serve as a pall bearer at a loved one's funeral. Why? Because true friends are there in the hard times as well as the good. In fact, I would argue that we can't truly know a friend intimately until we've walked with them through a trial.

Yet, when it comes to our friendship with God, many of us try to do just that. We want to share in God's glory, but we want to

20. Teresa of Avila, *Collected Works.*
21. Dan 6:10.
22. Luke 5:16.
23. Mark 1:35.
24. John 3:16.

bypass his Son's suffering. Scripture informs us that this isn't an option. Addressing the early Christians scattered in and around Asia Minor (modern-day Turkey), Peter attempts to convey this important aspect of friendship with God:

> Beloved, do not be surprised at the fiery ordeal among you, which comes upon you for your testing, as though some strange thing were happening to you; but to the degree that you *share the sufferings of Christ,* keep on rejoicing . . .[25]

What concerned Peter two thousand years ago should still concern the church today. Too many believers, young in their faith, wilt at the first sign of trouble. Their first encounter with Christ comes in power, so they're surprised when they experience pain. And who can blame them? In an attempt to fill pews, the modern church has largely neglected the task of discipleship. As a result, a generation of Christians has not been taught to "count the cost" of their faith.[26] Peter knew that for believers to hold fast, their introduction to Jesus couldn't rest solely on the power of persuasion. It had to be steeped in the sobriety of his suffering. To know Christ is to know him crucified.[27]

This is a message that is woefully under-preached in churches today. If you are a pastor reading this (especially a pastor specializing in youth or discipleship ministry), I implore you to teach this passage to those God has placed in your care. My aim is not for you to scare them; it's to prepare them. Friendship with God is a glorious thing, but glory isn't the only part of it. Knowing Christ, *truly* knowing him, requires that we know him in his suffering:

> . . . suffering and glory are a package that cannot be separated because they come from the same divine source. Jesus knew both. Thus, to have one without the other amounts to an incomplete knowledge of Jesus because

25. 1 Pet 4:12–13, emphasis mine.
26. Luke 14:28, ESV.
27. 1 Cor 2:2.

that was not the life that He lived. Again I say, that was
not the life that He lived![28]

The more complete our knowledge of our friends, the more
completely we can love them. A complete knowledge of Jesus
requires that we share in his suffering. Friendship with him isn't
always easy. Along the way it will cost us something. It might even
cost us everything. But the suffering we share pales in comparison
to the glory we will enjoy.[29]

Shared Celebration

Good friends are there for each other in times of trouble. They're
also there for each other in times of celebration. One of the great
privileges of friendship is the opportunity to share in another's joy.
Shared celebration gives friendship its sweetness. It's the reason we
smile whenever a good friend's name is mentioned in conversation.
It's also one of the things we miss most when a friend is forced to
say goodbye.

I've been richly blessed by the friends in my life, many of whom
I met in college. When school was over, four of us found ourselves
single and living in the Des Moines metro. Naturally, we thought
it would be more fun to live together than to live by ourselves, so
when one of my friends decided to purchase his first home, the rest
of us decided to move in! I spent most of my middle twenties living
in that four-person bachelor pad, nearly four years in total.

I look back fondly on those years for two simple reasons. We
celebrated a lot, and we celebrated together. We celebrated when
one of us got a new job or a promotion at work. We celebrated when
one of us had a birthday. We celebrated the start of a new baseball
or football season. We celebrated when the musician among us and
his band got a gig. We celebrated when one of us started dating
someone new. We *really* celebrated when one of us eventually got
engaged or married. And sometimes we simply celebrated that we'd
survived another week.

28. Lee, "Surprising Source of Joy."

29. 2 Cor 4:17.

Friendship is cause for rejoicing. Friendship with Jesus even more so. Throughout Scripture, those who came into contact with Christ, and realized exactly who he was, couldn't help but rejoice. And for one New Testament character, the rejoicing started early.[30] John the Baptist always understood who Jesus was, and what his role in their friendship should be. His followers were slower to catch on. Near the end of his life, his disciples grew alarmed over the decline of his ministry due to the growing ministry of Christ. But John admonished them to reconsider the source of their joy:

> "You yourselves are my witnesses that I said, 'I am not the Christ,' but, 'I have been sent ahead of Him.' He who has the bride is the bridegroom; but the friend of the bridegroom, who stands and hears him, rejoices greatly because of the bridegroom's voice. So this joy of mine has been made full."[31]

John understood that at a wedding, the main attraction is the bride and groom. The job of a groomsman is to share in the day's joy, not to be the focus of it. For John, joy was not to be found in the number of people he baptized; it was to be found in friendship with Christ. As friends of Jesus, we get a front row seat at the greatest party the world will ever know: the marriage feast of Christ and his church. We get to share in his celebration. What does sharing in this celebration look like? In a word: worship. And those who have friendship with Jesus are never without cause to worship.

We worship when he blesses us with a new day. We worship as we take in the beauty of his creation. We worship when we are reminded of the promises found in his word. We worship when we hear someone's testimony. We worship when we reflect on what he's done in our life. We worship when we experience grace. We worship when we witness his kingdom grow. And we worship when the lost get saved. The list goes on and on, but the point is this: our friendship with God grows when we celebrate with him.

---

30. Luke 1:41.

31. John 3:28–29.

Shared Conflict

Inevitably, no matter how well two friends get along, they will experience conflict. Sometimes it may amount to nothing more than a simple misunderstanding. Other times, it may lead to a knockdown, drag-out affair that devolves into a full-on feud. But the beautiful thing about friendship is this: when two friends work to resolve their differences, their friendship becomes stronger than if they had never found conflict at all.

Unfortunately, beautiful friendships are too often casualties of a failure to manage conflict well. This is a shame because the Bible gives us a pretty simple framework for working through conflict. It involves:

1. Confession (on the part of the offender)[32]
2. Repentance (on the part of the offender)[33]
3. Forgiveness (on the part of the offended)[34]

That's it. These three simple commands are absolutely crucial to ensuring friendship survives the wounds inflicted by the parties involved. Yet, in my observation they often go unheeded for two reasons. The first is sinful pride.[35] Offenders don't like to admit their offense, and those who have been offended find it hard to give up a grudge. Satan knows this and will do everything in his power to goad us into preserving our ego at the expense of repairing a rift. We must pray that God grants us hearts of humility so that we don't lose friendships to one of the oldest (and most effective) of the enemy's schemes.

The second reason we don't heed God's commands for resolving conflict is that many of us simply don't know how. Our society has lost what I call the "art of apology." When we fail to confess wrongdoing, we rob the offended party of a desperately needed olive branch. It's much more difficult to forgive when the

32. 1 John 1:9.
33. Luke 17:3-4.
34. 1 John 1:9 (again).
35. Prov 16:18.

offending party refuses to acknowledge their transgression. When we fail to confess wrongdoing, we also fail to model a behavior that the next generation desperately needs to see lived out if they're to have a shot at enjoying healthy friendships. And sadly, this behavior seems to get modeled less the higher one climbs the ladder of leadership and success.

Let me share a personal observation here. I have been working in a professional office setting for the entirety of my career, nearly twenty years in total. I've worked in higher education, as well as in the technology, insurance, and manufacturing industries. In all that time, across all of those industries, I can honestly say that I can count on one hand the number of times I've heard a sincere apology from a senior level leader. And this absence of apology isn't confined to corporate America. The art of apology has disappeared from the classrooms of our schools, the halls of our government, and in too many cases, even the sanctuaries of our churches. Think about it, when was the last time you heard a leader offer a sincere and heartfelt apology? How many times does a *mea culpa* contain more rationalization than remorse?

Somewhere along the line our society got the notion that once you've attained a certain amount of success or risen to a certain level of prominence or prestige; apologies are beneath you. This couldn't be further from the truth, or more incompatible with what the Bible says about how we should handle conflict. It's also the cause of unspeakable damage to the friendships in our lives.

We desperately need examples of penitence modeled by power. The moist poignant one I'm familiar with happened on July 3, 1863. The scene was Gettysburg, Pennsylvania. General Robert E. Lee, the Confederate commander, stood at the head of seventy-five thousand troops. Since 1861 he had, both literally and figuratively, outflanked the more numerous and better supplied Union army at nearly every turn. His confidence was brimming, and it showed as he formed his battle plans for the day. Dismissing the pleas of General James Longstreet to regroup on more advantageous terrain, Lee was determined to deploy a frontal assault across open ground in the hopes of splitting the center of General George Meade's Union forces . The strategy could not have yielded more disastrous results.

General George Pickett, tasked with leading the attack, charged away from the rebel ranks with roughly ten thousand men. Minutes later he returned with fewer than half who had not been killed or wounded in the ill-advised assault.

> As the minority who hadn't been cut to ribbons streamed back to the Confederate lines, Lee rode in . . . among them, apologizing. "It's all my fault," he assured stunned privates and corporals . . . "I am very sorry—the task was too great for you." . . . After Gettysburg, Lee never mounted another murderous head-on assault.[36]

General Lee was the most revered figure of the Confederacy. He was adored by southerners and worshipped by his troops. But on that suffocating summer day in 1863, he found himself mournfully confessing fault to a tattered band of bleeding and sobbing soldiers, most of whom did not rank high enough to care for his horse. The scene is striking for both the humanity and humility displayed.

Robert E. Lee remains one of the more enigmatic figures in American history. Admirers and critics of his legacy abound. But regardless of one's view of him, it's clear that on that pivotal day in the war between the states, Lee demonstrated what God looks for in a sincere apology: a broken and contrite spirit.[37]

This is a crucial attitude to cultivate in our friendship with God. As fallen creatures, we are always the offenders when conflict arises with him. As a holy God, he is always the offended. On the surface this may seem a one-sided, untenable dynamic that would prove detrimental to friendship. After all, if one party is always right and the other always wrong, there's no way the friendship can last, right? But this is precisely where friendship with God is such a comforting thing. If we do our part, namely the confessing and repenting of our sin, he is *always* faithful to do his:

> If we confess our sins, He is faithful and righteous to forgive us our sins and to cleanse us from all unrighteousness.[38]

36. Blount, "Making Sense of Lee."
37. Ps 51:17.
38. 1 John 1:9.

The very best of our earthly friends will nearly always forgive us, but they are powerless to cleanse us. God is a friend who is always willing and able to do both. It's this dynamic that makes friendship with God not just tenable, but eternal.

THE EVIDENCE OF FRIENDSHIP

Preference for Pals

We've covered how friendships are born, as well as how they grow. Now let's cover how they are perceived. Friendships don't exist in a vacuum. They're lived out in public. The world can't help but notice that a friendship exists based on the words, actions, and priorities of the individuals who share it. Every friendship leaves evidence of its existence. And that evidence has an impact on others, whether they participate in that particular friendship or not.

The first piece of evidence that suggests friendship exists between two or more individuals is that they prefer each other's company. All things considered, friends prefer to be with each other more than they prefer to be with others. This stands to reason given what we've already said about the birth and growth of friendship. Let me use an example from my pre-fatherhood days. For a few years spanning my late twenties, I had a standing tee time with some of my friends from church. Every Wednesday night we would convene at a local municipal golf course and play nine holes. We took part in this weekly ritual from early April to late October for two simple reasons: we preferred golf, and we preferred each other's company.

I suspect we also preferred it because it served as a petri dish of sorts for growing our friendship. It provided a common interest (the game of golf), shared revelation (you learn a lot about someone's character in a game where you call penalties on yourself), shared communication (friendly banter between shots), shared suffering (abundant bogeys), shared celebration (rare birdies), and even shared conflict (inconsistent knowledge of the rules led to many on-course debates).

If you had asked for observations on our group from any of the other golfers we let play through, they probably would've said two things. First, they would've made it clear that none of us were in danger of being invited to play in the next year's Masters. Second, they would've commented on how much the members of our group seemed to enjoy each other.

Like a single golfer playing through a foursome, the world can't help but notice the friendships going on around them. As Christians, they should notice our friendship with God. And the evidence of our friendship should start with our preference for being with him. The apostle Paul conveyed this preference in the strongest of terms when he wrote to the Corinthians that he would "prefer rather to be absent from the body and to be at home with the Lord."[39]

While Paul's stated preference will eventually be granted to every Christian upon their death (or Christ's return), in the meantime we should cultivate habits that show the world our preference for being with God. Not for show, but because we genuinely desire to feel close to our Savior. Do your words indicate to others your preference for Jesus? Your actions? Your priorities? Your money? Your time? If the answer is no, I invite you to take a prayerful break from reading this book and ask God to help you cultivate a preference for him.

Faithfulness

A second piece of evidence that suggests friendship exists is the demonstration of faithfulness. Good friends are there through thick and thin. They honor their shared history with their steadfastness. When adversity strikes, friends are there to help. When enemies attack, friends are there to defend. When health falters, friends are there to nurse. When hearts are broken, friends are there to console. Friends don't discard each other for someone more attractive when the ugliness of life sets in. They use that ugliness as an opportunity to demonstrate the depth of their friendship.

39. 2 Cor 5:8b.

The same is true of friendship with God. What could sever our friendship with him? What would cause him to choose another over us? According to the apostle Paul, nothing:

> Who will separate us from the love of Christ? Will tribulation, or distress, or persecution, or famine, or nakedness, or peril, or sword? . . . For I am convinced that neither death, nor life, nor angels, nor principalities, nor things present, nor things to come, nor powers, nor height, nor depth, nor any other created thing, will be able to separate us from the love of God, which is in Christ Jesus our Lord.[40]

In God, we find the most faithful of friends. So faithful, in fact, that he supplies the devotion needed on both ends of our friendship with him. Calvinist theologians refer to this dynamic of God's friendship with us as the *perseverance of the saints*. The idea is that those whom God calls to truly be his friends will not fail to persevere in in their faith until he calls them home. While I heartily affirm this tenet of Reformed theology, I think I prefer R. C. Sproul's alternative phrasing: *preservation of the saints*.[41] God knows that as fickle, fallen creatures we struggle with faithfulness in our friendship with him. We sinners are quick to trade fidelity to him for worldly comforts found elsewhere. That is why he sent his Spirit to help *preserve* the faithfulness needed on our end to maintain our friendship with him.[42] So the next time you find yourself thanking God for his faithfulness, don't forget to thank him for yours.

Sacrifice

Another piece of evidence that suggests friendship exists is when we witness sacrifice on the part of one individual for another. Friendship, by its very nature, is selfless. Good friends will give you a ride. Great friends will give you a kidney. The measure of a friendship is often marked by the size of the sacrifices made.

40. Rom 8:35, 38–39.
41. Sproul, "TULIP."
42. John 14:16.

I've been blessed with many great friends in my life who have sacrificed much on my behalf. One of the most meaningful sacrifices was made by one of my old college roommates, Andrew. In the summer of 2008, I was engaged to be married, and I had asked Andrew to serve as one of my groomsmen. This was no small favor to ask as Andrew had re-located to Florida after having recently graduated from chiropractic school and was struggling to get his fledgling practice off the ground. A trip back to Iowa would require the expense of a plane ticket, hotel stay, tux rental, and all of the other incidentals that come with being a member of a wedding party. Not exactly what your financial advisor wants to hear as you struggle to dig out from under a mountain of school and small business loans. But Andrew was a good friend and knew that I would gladly repay the favor should he ever get married, so he eagerly booked his trip.

A couple of months before the big day, I made a tearful call to Andrew to tell him that the wedding had been postponed. Shortly after I had gotten engaged, I had begun to notice a troubling lack of energy, which soon morphed into an emotional numbness that I knew was very uncharacteristic of a man about to married. The numbness gave way to despair and after an initially missed diagnosis I was eventually told by doctors that I was suffering from a severe case of clinical depression. I was in no shape to get out of bed, let alone walk down the aisle, and so I made the most difficult decision of my life: to postpone my wedding. Andrew took this all in stride and since his flight was non-refundable, offered to visit me in Iowa that summer as originally planned. Our weekend together was certainly a blessing to me, but it must have been difficult for him to look into the hollow eyes of a friend who'd had the joy snuffed out of his life.

A few months later, thanks to the persistent prayers of loved ones and with help from some amazing mental health professionals, I had recovered enough for my fiancée (now wife) and I to set a new date for our wedding. What was originally planned to be a summer affair had been rescheduled for the week before Christmas. I called Andrew to let him know the happy news, albeit with a heavy heart. Given his circumstances, I did not expect him to make a return trip and I told him as much over the phone. It was then that he responded with four words I'll never forget, "McConnell, I'll be there."

Being a good friend requires sacrifice. Friendship with God requires no less. Sometimes the sacrifices are small, like showing up early to church to greet newcomers or staying late to stack chairs. Other times, the sacrifices are larger, like using the money you had saved for a new car to adopt an orphan or burning a year's worth of accrued vacation time to attend a church planting bootcamp. But no matter the size or frequency of our sacrifices, the apostle John makes it clear what the gold standard is for sacrificial friendship:

> Greater love has no one than this, that one lay down his life for his friends.[43]

We will never find a greater friend than Jesus because we will never find a friend willing to sacrifice more for our friendship. He gave his life on the cross to demonstrate, not only to us, but to the world his love for us. Friendship does not get any more evident than that.

Fruit

A beautiful thing happens over time when friends (who are friends for the right reasons) continue to show preference for one another, remain faithful to one another, and sacrifice for one another. Eventually their friendship can't help but positively impact the world around them. Let me use an example from my college days. About a month into my freshman year at the University of Northern Iowa, I joined Sigma Phi Epsilon fraternity. A month prior I'd had absolutely zero interest in Greek life. My only exposure to fraternities had been via the movie *Animal House*, and my dad's stories from his own days as a fraternity man at Iowa State. To be honest, neither source had done a good job marketing what fraternity life had to offer.

But the offer of free food and fellowship is a powerful draw for a hungry and lonely freshman trying to find his way on a campus of

---

43. John 15:13.

thirteen thousand people. After enjoying a burnt burger and some friendly banter with the SigEps on the front lawn of 818 West Seerley Boulevard, I concluded two things: these guys were pretty fun, and they appeared to live their lives according to principles I could affirm. The rest, as they say, is history.

A funny thing happened over the next four years. What started out as a way to meet people and have a little fun evolved into a lifestyle that benefited not only myself, but the campus and civic communities. On a Monday afternoon, my fraternity brothers and I might find ourselves playing intramural softball. On Tuesday, we would be reading to school children at a local elementary. On Wednesday, we might convene for an impromptu video game night. On Thursday, we would hold a date auction with all proceeds benefiting a local women's shelter. On Friday night, we might hit a local dance club. On Saturday morning, we'd be cleaning up roadside trash on a local highway. As friendship grows it yields more than just fun; it yields fruit.

Our friendship with God is no different. In the same chapter where he reveals to us our identity as his friends, Jesus also reveals to us what evidence of his friendship looks like:

> Abide in Me, and I in you. As the branch cannot bear fruit of itself unless it abides in the vine, so neither can you unless you abide in Me. I am the vine, you are the branches; *he who abides in Me and I in him, he bears much fruit*, for apart from Me you can do nothing.[44]

As we grow in our friendship with Jesus, not only are we afforded opportunities to enjoy him for who he is, but we are afforded opportunities to bear fruit. And the wonderful thing about the fruit of godly friendship is that the impact is felt not merely by the campus or the community, but by the kingdom of God. God does not need our help to expand his kingdom, but like any good friend he looks for ways to include us in his pursuits. Apart from him, we are lonely freshman trying to find our way. But God is like a BMOC (Big Man On Campus) who seeks us out between classes

44. John 15:4–5, emphasis mine.

and invites us to hang with him that weekend. His friendship not only means the world but changes it.

Friendship is one of the greatest joys to be found in life. Keeping company with close friends provides a sweet satisfaction that has few rivals this side of heaven. Like a thick blanket on a cold winter day, time spent with friends provides comfort, warmth, and security. And like a blanket suddenly pulled away, the loss of friendship is an experience that is both cold and cruel.

One of the aforementioned fraternity brothers I met my freshman year had a saying that I've always loved. He'd say, "Guys, friends are for reasons, seasons, or life; and this, this is for life." With God we add a fourth category to this nifty classification system for friendship. With God we find a friend for eternity.

It's this quality of friendship that meant so much to Job. As he laments the loss of his prime, it's not the deterioration of his health or the disappearance of his wealth that has him broken. It's the apparent loss of his friendship with God. You see, Job knew that living life in one's prime isn't truly possible without the friendship of God. Sure, we may enjoy seasons of blessing along the way that feel like our prime, but we can never feel anything approaching the full weight of God's glory without first enjoying the intimacy of friendship with our Savior.

At the beginning of this chapter I compared the friendship of God to the roux, the main ingredient, in a batch of gumbo. The recipe simply doesn't work without it, and neither does living life in our prime. But just like gumbo, other ingredients are necessary for prime living. Let's take a look at what goes into the pot next.

Consecrated Kids

...And my children were with me.

—JOB 29:5B

In keeping with my gumbo analogy, it's time to move on to the next ingredient in our recipe for prime living. As we covered in the last chapter, the key to a good batch is in the roux. And Job teaches us that the key to living life in one's prime is friendship with God. But what's next? In a batch of gumbo, once the roux has reached its desired hue, the triumvirate of onion, celery, and pepper (along with a healthy dose of garlic) is quickly added and stirred for a couple minutes to ensure the flavors meld together properly. Next, it's time to add in the meat of the dish. And when it comes to gumbo, three sources of animal protein are called for. The first of which is diced chicken breast. I prefer to add it at this stage so it can start cooking along with the veggies. The roux, which by now has reached a saucy consistency, naturally adheres itself to the chicken and infuses it with flavor. This is the best time to be standing over the pot as the fragrance of sautéing veggies and roux-cooked chicken begins to fill the kitchen. It's the sort of smell that permeates your clothes and clings to your hair. But you don't mind so much when you know what awaits your taste buds at the end of this culinary adventure.

Just like our batch of gumbo, Job mentions three elements that served as the "meat" of the prime of his life. After his friendship with God, they were the things he missed most after Satan had been given permission to take a wrecking ball to his life. And the first of these was the presence of his children. The only thing painful enough to be mentioned in the same verse as the perceived loss of his friendship with God was the actual loss of his children.

On some level we should expect that Job's discourse would go here next. In Job 29 we find a man crushed with grief. All of his children had been killed in a freak accident. He had no warning. He had no way to save them. He had no time to say goodbye. As a parent, I can't imagine how anyone in Job's situation could've moved on, let alone found the strength to take another step. When people talk of losing the will to live, it's circumstances like these they have in mind. But even in the midst of so much death, Job has a lesson for our life.

TIME IS NOT ON OUR SIDE

As a parent of young children, I receive a lot of compliments on the cuteness of my kids.[1] I also receive a lot of unsolicited parenting advice. The advice takes many forms but often ends with a familiar admonition to, "enjoy them while they're little because they grow up so darned fast." I used to brush off comments like this, but as I continue to hear them time and time again, I realize there are really only two ways you can take them:

1. As mere moments of nostalgia, triggered by your children and verbalized in your presence

2. As the voice of wisdom on repeat

I've decided to go with the latter. Some lessons are best learned through experience. And experienced parents will tell you that the time you have with your children is limited. Whether it's dropping them off at college, waving goodbye to a bus headed for basic training, moving them to a new city for their first job, or in the tragic case of Job, laying them to rest, a day will come when the time we have to parent our children will run out. Are we stewarding it wisely? We'd

---

1. Usually from people who weren't awake with them at 2 a.m. that morning.

better be, because in half a verse Job makes it abundantly clear that it is essential to living life in our prime.

Yet, when it comes to spending time with our kids, I'm amazed at how willing parents are to forfeit this precious and finite resource. Why? Well, there's enough to chew on there to fill another book. And as a parent whose kids aren't yet half raised, I don't claim to be an authority on the subject. But let me share a few observations about what may be encroaching on the time we spend with our kids.

Let me start with demographics. Today's parents are becoming parents later than ever before. According to research,[2] the average age of first-time mothers in the U.S. in 1970 was just over twenty-one. Today, it's over twenty-six. In and of itself, that's not a bad thing. In fact, there are some real benefits to waiting to have children. Older parents are generally more mature. They are typically more financially stable. For those who are married, they've oftentimes had an opportunity to grow in their marriage without the stress of raising young children.

These are all healthy things. But they also beg the question, if today's young people aren't having kids in their early twenties, how are they investing that time? As I observe my generational peers, I see them devoting themselves primarily to two things: careers and hobbies. Again, in and of themselves, neither of these is a bad thing. Our careers are important. Since the beginning, God has created us for work.[3] There is dignity in work because the creative process we employ on the job points to the character of the Creator. There is purpose in our work because it provides a public platform for living out our faith.

Our careers are important, but the old adage that "all work and no play makes Jack a dull boy," continues to ring true. Hobbies are also important. God's creation is an incredible playground and God loves to see his children at play. If you want a fun, out-of-the-box Bible study, search the Scriptures and explore the theology of leisure. Hobbies help refresh us and provide points of common

2. Bichell, "Average Age."
3. Gen 2:15.

interest. And as we covered in the last chapter, this can lead to the birth of friendship.

Careers and hobbies are good, but as any good parent can tell you, when children come along, the time (and energy) we have available to devote to both decreases. While we still need to make a living and enjoy some periods of leisure from time to time, parenthood requires that on some level we place both our careers and our hobbies on the alter. Sadly, these are sacrifices that too few are willing to make. Why? Let me suggest two reasons.

First, the longer we wait to have kids, the harder it is to give things up for them. This is a dynamic that I feel is more pronounced for my generation. Many of my peers didn't start having kids until their late twenties. I was thirty-one when I brought my oldest son home. Others wait even longer. A lot of years passed between the time we left school and the day we became parents. And we filled those years with lots of things.

Some threw themselves into their careers. They worked long hours, spent their nights and weekends in MBA classes, and climbed the corporate ladder. Others used their freedom and disposable income to travel extensively or devote themselves to their hobbies. Some did all of the above. And something happened along the way that didn't happen to the same degree to the generations that came before us. These things became harder to let go of.

If you've spent your twenties and early thirties climbing to the level of senior management, it's harder for you to decline your CEO's offer to join the board of directors than it is for the twenty-two-year-old, entry-level associate whom the CEO couldn't pick out of a lineup. Likewise, if you've spent each of the last nine years attending spring training in Florida with your buddies, it's harder for you to miss out on year ten than the guy who's never seen a Grapefruit League game. As self-centered sinners, sacrificing things we've invested years in to spend time in the presence of our children is hard. It's harder still when the things we're giving up have been such a big part of our lives for such a long time.

Second, our role in the workplace often offers a much more consistent source of recognition and praise than our role as a parent. Think about it. If you show up on time, treat your peers and superiors with respect, and churn out quality work, sooner or later any employer worth working for will recognize you for your effort. It might be in the form of a word of thanks, a spot reward, a raise, or maybe even a promotion. These things feel good, especially when they're received in the place where we spend the majority of our waking hours.

On the other hand, if you pass on that promotion so that you can get home early on Wednesdays to lead your child's youth group, volunteer to take the night shift with your colicky infant so your spouse can get some sleep, or patiently correct your strong-willed three-year-old for the ninth time this morning, your reward will most likely sound like a chorus of crickets.

Our society (and sadly, this includes our churches) does a poor job of providing recognition for the sacrifices necessary for good parenting. This self-defeating attitude desperately needs adjustment as our society is only as healthy as the families it's composed of. Each of us have a part to play in this, but I want to offer an exhortation to three specific parties:

Spouses

Unfortunately, the world will rarely (if ever) praise your husband/ wife for being a good parent. And so, you must. We all crave recognition in our pursuits. Don't let it be easier for your spouse to find appreciation in pursuing something other than being a good Mom or Dad.

Grandparents

You probably spent much of your own attention as a parent praising the achievements of your children. This was a good thing. Your kids needed to hear you were proud of them. But a transition in the way you praise your children needs to take place. As your children become parents themselves, they will face a daily choice between pursuing personal achievement and fulfilling their calling as parents. The subject of your praise will tell them which you value more.

Churches

God's word is very clear on the importance God places on parenting. Not only are children to be regarded as a gift from the Lord, but the task of raising them in a godly manner is so important that God includes it as a qualification for leadership in his church.[4] Yet, when it comes time to select a new overseer, too many churches gloss over this requirement. As long as the children of the candidate aren't an obvious train wreck, we quickly check the box and move on. This doesn't do the candidate, or your church, any favors. Churches are a reflection of their leaders. And church leaders are called to reflect God's values when it comes to parenting. Like Job, do your leaders place a premium on the presence of their children? Have they ever sacrificed something to ensure they could spend more time with them (even if that thing was a healthy ministry opportunity)?

Perhaps the reason this requirement is adhered to so inconsistently is because it's the most difficult to verify. Most of the other qualifications for eldership can be observed publicly (monogamy, temperance, hospitality, gentleness, ability to teach, etc.). But the management of one's household happens mostly in private. So, what are churches to do?

Let me suggest a helpful practice I gleaned from a church plant I was part of several years ago. When it came time to select the church's first elders, the two pastors applied all of the scriptural criteria to their list of candidates. After selecting their finalists, they performed one final step. They called the wives of those they planned to invite to become elders. That phone call consisted of one simple question. After briefly reviewing the list of qualifications with the candidate's spouse, they asked, "Do you have any hesitation concerning your husband becoming an elder?" This single question affords a peak behind the curtain into the home life of the candidate in question. And if that candidate is in the midst of raising children, the response carries even more weight. Why? Because the best judge of the priority one places on parenting is often the other parent.

4. Ps 127:3–5; 1 Tim 3:4–5.

Today's generation of parents faces challenges on every front. Perhaps none more so than the temptation to trade time with their children for career accolades or more pleasurable pursuits. After all, a quiet morning spent fishing with friends looks a lot more attractive than a hectic afternoon spent untangling the lines of your kids. But this is a temptation we must resist. Job paints a portrait that conveys a sobering reality. Our time with our children is limited. Living life in our prime demands we make the most of it.

THUS JOB DID CONTINUALLY

The lesson we must glean from Job's grief is to cherish the time we have with our children. And while it's a lesson that requires daily reminders, it can be learned. And speaking from personal experience, it's a lesson that's easier learned early. As I awaited the arrival of my oldest son, I knew that in order to be the father that God wanted me to be, I would have to give up a few things. For me that started with two dearly loved hobbies that I had pursued since I was a teenager: bow hunting and golf. Both are wonderful pastimes. But both require two things that are in much shorter supply when you become a father: time and money. So, since November 1, 2012, the day I became a father, I've not climbed into a deer stand. Golf seasons that used to exceed eighteen rounds, in recent years have not surpassed eighteen holes.[5]

And I'm not alone. Refreshingly, many in my generation have done the same. Research shows that today's fathers spend nearly triple the time caring for their children than fathers of preceding generations. "Today's mothers spend more time with their children than mothers did in the 1960s."[6] But prioritizing time with our children is only half the battle. The other half is figuring out how we should use that time. Here again, Job offers a template. But we must rewind his story back to chapter 1. How did Job focus the time he had with his children?

5. Don't make me out to be a saint or an ascetic just yet. I'm still known to frequent a fishing hole from time to time.
6. Pew Research Center, *Modern Parenthood*.

His sons used to go and hold a feast in the house of each one on his day, and they would send and invite their three sisters to eat and drink with them. When the days of feasting had completed their cycle, Job would send and consecrate them, rising up early in the morning and offering burnt offerings according to the number of them all; for Job said, "Perhaps my sons have sinned and cursed God in their hearts." Thus Job did continually.[7]

When it came to his kids, Job's primary concern was for their relationship with God. This shouldn't be surprising given that he viewed friendship with God as paramount to the prime of his own life. Serving as his family's priest, Job would continually offer up sacrifices on their behalf on the off chance that they had sinned during one of their weekly celebrations. The text also tells us that Job would send and consecrate them. The word *consecrate* is not one we generally use in everyday discourse, so I think it's important that we define it. The word essentially means to set apart for a special or sacred purpose. I can't think of a more appropriate term to provide clarity about how we should focus the time we have with our kids. When it comes to our children, the time we spend with them is always a means to an end. The question is, for what purpose are we setting them apart?

For a practical example of what this should look like, I think it's helpful to examine a very famous father and son. Of all the kings of Israel, King David was the one with a heart most pleasing to God. His son, Solomon, was the king who enjoyed the most success. This was no accident. As a father, David was very intentional about the purpose for which he was setting his son apart:

David said, "My son Solomon is young and inexperienced, and the house that is to be built for the LORD shall be exceedingly magnificent, famous and glorious throughout all lands. Therefore now I will make preparation for it." So David made ample preparations before his death. Then he called for his son Solomon, and charged him to build a house for the LORD God of Israel. . . . "Now, my son, the LORD be with you that you may be

7. Job 1:4–5.

successful, and build the house of the LORD your God just as He has spoken concerning you. Only the LORD give you discretion and understanding, and give you charge over Israel, so that you may keep the law of the LORD your God. Then you will prosper, if you are careful to observe the statutes and the ordinances which the LORD commanded Moses concerning Israel. Be strong and courageous, do not fear nor be dismayed. Now behold, with great pains I have prepared for the house of the LORD 100,000 talents of gold and 1,000,000 talents of silver, and bronze and iron beyond weight, for they are in great quantity; also timber and stone I have prepared, and you may add to them. Moreover, there are many workmen with you, stonecutters and masons of stone and carpenters, and all men who are skillful in every kind of work. Of the gold, the silver and the bronze and the iron there is no limit. Arise and work, and may the LORD be with you." David also commanded all the leaders of Israel to help his son Solomon . . .[8]

Solomon had a very important job to do. The lynchpin of his legacy as king of Israel would be the successful construction of the temple in Jerusalem. It would be his primary means of glorifying God. His father, David, knew this. And as a result, he took great pains to put key elements in place as he consecrated his son for this work.

A Child's Charge

David made it a point to provide Solomon with a charge concerning the construction of the temple. As parents, we want our children to glorify God, but we are sometimes a little vague with our encouragement. Our kids need to be reminded that they "were created by His purpose, and for His purpose."[9] God may not reveal your child's calling as early or as specifically as he did with David and Solomon. But that doesn't absolve us from our responsibility as parents to instill in our children that they have one. God has a job that only

8. 1 Chr 22:5–6, 11–17.
9. Warren, *The Purpose Driven Life*, 17.

your child can accomplish. Much of the work of parenting lies in praying for discernment concerning how your child's God-granted giftedness can help them accomplish it. Helping your child marry their gifts to God-glorifying opportunities to use them is one of the great joys of parenthood. Make sure you don't miss out on it.

Wisdom, Obedience, Courage

Providing our kids with a charge to glorify God is a good first step. But by itself it's not enough to ensure any sort of success. A godly charge must be propped up with prayer and instruction. David knew that for Solomon to succeed in building the temple, he would need more than a well-articulated mission. He would also need a well-articulated character. As David prays for and exhorts his son, note the things he mentions are going to be necessary for Solomon to be successful in his charge:

- Discretion and understanding (wisdom)
- Keeping the law (obedience)
- Strength and courage

As you pray for your children, are these character traits top of mind? Are you on the lookout for teachable moments in your child's life where you can impart wisdom? Are you teaching them a love for and obedience to God's word? Are you parenting in a way that's more *en*couraging than *dis*couraging? If you're anything like me, answering these questions quickly becomes an exercise in confession and repentance. But I want to let you in on a little secret. Your kids will often give you more grace than you feel you deserve as a parent. And God will always give you more grace than you feel you deserve as a person. In this we should take heart, and heed King David's advice.

Great Pains

Next, David goes on to recount for Solomon the great pains he's taken to prepare him for success. The amount of gold, silver, iron, bronze, timber, and stone that David had amassed for the temple's construction would boggle the mind of any builder. And his preparations weren't limited to providing material goods. He had also lined up workmen possessing every skill necessary to ensure the temple was built precisely to specifications.

Like David, many parents will take great pains to ensure their child's success. The question is, do the pains taken contribute to God's charge for your child, or the world's? I'm continually amazed at the amount of time, energy, and money poured into extracurricular activities by today's parents. The opportunities are endless. Little League, swim lessons, soccer club, drama camp, after-school art program, flag football, basketball, and Lego club are but a sample of the fliers that have made their way home this year in my son's backpack. And he's only in first grade! And all of this in the hopes of starting our kids down the path to success.

Am I advocating that we shun involvement in after-school activities? No. If your child has good hand-eye coordination and an affinity for sunflower seeds, sign them up for baseball. They'll benefit from the camaraderie and teamwork inherent in that sport. If your child's dialogue during imaginative play rivals the script of the latest Star Wars film, sign them up for drama camp. They'll benefit from the creative outlet and art of storytelling found on stage.

But I start to get a little queasy when I see six-year-olds who are dual sport athletes . . . in the same season. I worry when I see kindergarteners whose travel schedule rivals that of club teams at the collegiate level. Will these kids enjoy more success in these pursuits than their peers who don't devote the same amount of time? Maybe. But at what cost?

Navigating these waters as a parent isn't easy. The pull of the world is a strong one. At times, the opportunities available to our children constitute an embarrassment of riches. How should we choose among them? How much time should we devote to them? How much do they complement or compete with my child's spiritual growth? In his book, *Your Days Are Numbered*, John Perritt offers a wise admonition as we consider these questions:

Extra-curricular activities are often the major factor which hinders the spiritual growth of children. Let's give our children the opportunities to participate in the traveling drama club or excel musically with their voice, but start by telling the culture how much time they can have our children instead of the other way around.[10]

I like to tease my wife that we have a lot of FOMO (Fear Of Missing Out) in our house. We love to be involved in both our church and our community. When a situation arises where we're forced to miss out on something, it can trigger a brief moment of sadness for one or more of the members of our family. While our FOMO can sometimes get out of hand, it can also prove useful when channeled in the proper way. King David feared that his son might miss out on fulfilling the charge God had placed on his life. As a result, he took great pains to do everything in his power to ensure Solomon succeeded. My prayer is that a "holy FOMO" pesters each one of us as we take pains to ensure the success of our own children as they pursue God's charge for their lives. Missing out on that is something truly worth fearing.

Recruiting Help

Speaking of Solomon, he seems to have inherited more from his father than a well-organized bill of materials. He also inherited his dad's advisors. At the end of the passage in 1 Chronicles quoted above, David tells us he also "commanded all the leaders of Israel to help his son." David knew that the job his son faced was not one that should be tackled alone. Solomon would need the advice and practical help of others as he worked to fulfill God's charge for his life. I have no doubt the assistance of Israel's leaders was crucial to his successfully completing the temple. And I'll venture a guess that it may have been this dynamic that Solomon had in mind when he penned the following proverb:

10. Perritt, *Your Days Are Numbered*, 126.

Without consultation, plans are frustrated, but with many counselors they succeed.[11]

Just as in the example of David and Solomon, the work of consecrating our children for the charge God has placed on their lives is not one that should be tackled alone. Even well-intentioned, prayerful parents with healthy motivations will have blind spots. The lessons learned from our own life experiences will not always be a sufficient reference as we seek to advise our children. Therefore, we must recruit some help. We need to prayerfully consider who in our lives can help provide godly counsel to our children. And once we've identified who these people are, we need to formally invite them to invest in our children's lives. Without their help, we invite frustration. But with their counsel, we invite success.

A WORD TO THOSE WITHOUT CHILDREN

I realize it may seem like I've spent the bulk of this chapter writing directly to parents. If you don't have children and you're still reading this, thanks for sticking with me. I'm convinced that God has something for you in this half verse from Job too. Kids are certainly not a prerequisite for experiencing the prime of life. If they were, Jesus himself would've been disqualified. The fact of the matter is, certain aspects of parenthood aren't reserved solely for those who procreate. Take it from another Christian who didn't have kids:

To Timothy, my true child in the faith . . .[12]
To Timothy, beloved son . . .[13]

As the apostle Paul opens his letters to Timothy, he makes it abundantly clear that he considered himself to be the spiritual father of Timothy. The remainder of his letters to Timothy are full of instructions, warnings, encouragement, reminders, and advice conveying his care and concern for his son in the faith. It's this sort of spiritual parenthood that all followers of Christ should aspire

11. Prov 15:22.
12. 1 Tim 1:2.
13. 2 Tim 1:2.

to. For when we lead someone to a saving faith in Jesus, and/or are given the privilege of discipling them, we assume the role of a spiritual father or mother. It's a role full of joy . . . and responsibility. Like young children, Christians who are young in their faith need spiritual parents who are willing to:

- Make sacrifices in order to spend time with them.
- Help them find God's charge for their life.
- Impart wisdom, obedience, and courage from God's word.
- Take pains to ensure their success in God's kingdom.
- Recruit other godly men and women to counsel them along the way.

So, whether you are a biological, adoptive, foster, or spiritual parent, let us borrow an ingredient from Job's recipe for prime living. May we never take for granted the brief time we have with our children. And may we never fail to use that time to consecrate them for the charge God has placed on their lives. What Job did continually for his kids, Christ did conclusively for us. By virtue of his work on the cross, we are "consecrated kids" in his kingdom. Let us eagerly work to fulfill the charge he has for each of us. And let us eagerly look forward to the next ingredient for prime living Job has for us . . .

Butter And Oil

When my steps were bathed in butter, and
the rock poured out for me streams of oil!

—JOB 29:6

This will be a short chapter. Some things just don't need a lot of explanation. Like the penultimate ingredient in a batch of gumbo, the next thing on Job's list of items essential for prime living is easily processed. After the diced chicken has been sufficiently cooked in the delightfully fragrant roux mixture, several cups of chicken stock are added to the pot to give gumbo its soupy consistency. Next, it's time to add in the second of the dish's three meats. Andouille, a smoked and spiced sausage that can be purchased at most grocery stores, is sliced (or diced) and tossed into the pot. That's it. No additional prep is necessary. Just like that you're one ingredient away from covering the pot and focusing your attention elsewhere.

As Job reflects on the prime of his life, he moves past friendship with God and the presence of his children. In verse 6, he employs hyperbole to describe yet another aspect of his incredibly blessed life that had gone missing. Job begins the verse by recalling his steps as being "bathed in butter." What exactly does Job mean by this? First, we must remember from chapter 1 that Job was, among other things, the ancient world's equivalent of a cattle baron. His seven thousand camels would've produced an immense amount of milk for consumption or sale. It's plausible that he maintained at least a small herd of cattle not enumerated in Job 1 that also could've contributed to his burgeoning dairy operation. The famous English pastor and theologian, John Gill, commented that his livestock likely,

> produced such a vast quantity of milk, that when his servants brought it from the fields to the dairy, their milk pails ran over in such abundance, that Job could not step out of his house, and take a walk in his fields, but he stepped into puddles of milk, of which butter was made . . .[1]

In other words, for Job, business was good. Really good. Was he actually sidestepping puddles of milk on a daily basis? Probably not. But his exaggeration is meant to convey the simple fact that his was an embarrassment of riches. And the blessings weren't confined to his livestock. He extends the hyperbole to his farming operations. He ends verse 6 by telling us that "the rock poured out for me streams of oil." I'll admit, this is a bit of a confusing line for an Iowa boy who's spent most of his life surrounded by some of the world's most fertile black dirt. But in the ancient land of Uz, the rocky soil and Mediterranean climate must've been perfect for growing olives. Job's groves were so fruitful that even the rocks seemed to be pouring out oil for him.

Like an investment banker whose salary, bonus, and portfolio were all taking off, Job was experiencing material blessing on every front. Though not on par with the friendship of God or the presence of his children, he counts these blessings as another facet of the prime of his life. But we must be careful not to paint too rosy a picture. If you are looking for a "prosperity gospel" or "health and wealth" doctrine in this passage, this is where I burst your bubble. Job's incredible material success did not make him immune to trial or trouble. Even in the prime of his life, Job knew dark days. How do we know this? Because he said so himself:

> When His lamp shone over my head, And by His light I walked through darkness[2]

1. Gill, *Exposition of the Bible.*
2. Job 29:3.

Given our focus to this point, this verse seems almost out of place. But there it sits, just three verses prior in the text. Was Job blessed in greater measure than you or I will ever be with material wealth? Yes. Was he without a care in the world? No. It is crucial that we interpret this passage in a balanced manner. And the interpretation is this: the prime of Job's life was not characterized by an absence of darkness, but by the presence of God's light.

It's critical that we get this right as we evaluate the seasons of our own lives. Sometimes we can be led to believe the lie that unless *everything* is going well, God must be holding out on us. That simply isn't true. The most blessed man of his age gives testimony that the prime of our lives will not be void of trouble. In a fallen world, darkness comes, even in the best of times. But God never leaves us without a light. And he often holds it higher above our heads than we ever could.

See, I told you this would be a short chapter.

A Seat In The Square

When I went out to the gate of the city,
When I took my seat in the square . . .

—JOB 29:7

If you're tiring of my culinary metaphors, you need only stick with me for a couple more paragraphs. We've covered that like a well-rendered roux in a batch of gumbo, the friendship of God served as the foundation of Job's prime of life. And like diced chicken and andouille sausage, the blessings of children and material wealth made up the meat of his prime. Wrapping up this recipe requires sprinkling a liberal portion of your favorite Cajun seasoning and tossing in a bay leaf before covering the pot. But there's one final ingredient that rounds out the dish that mustn't be forgotten. In the final ten minutes of cooking, the recipe calls for the addition of a pound of shrimp.[1] Shrimp is easily overcooked, so you want to wait until nearly the end to add this bounty of the sea. The final ten minutes is just enough time to ensure the shrimp is cooked and has absorbed a little of the sumptuous flavor imparted by the rest of the ingredients.

Sadly, in my kitchen this capstone ingredient nearly always goes missing. Why? It's not because I'm a landlocked Iowan with no access to seafood (though it could definitely be fresher). No, this gross omission is the fault of my beautiful bride. When I asked her

1. Tails or no tails on the shrimp is the chef's call.

out on our first dinner date, I (wisely) asked her if there was any type of food she didn't eat. She politely, but firmly replied, "I don't eat anything that swims." As a result, my trips to seafood joints have been severely curbed. And my gumbo has been sans shrimp for the duration of our marriage.

Like eating a batch of gumbo without shrimp, it's hard to feel like we're enjoying life in its prime if there's a missing ingredient. And in our day and age, what's missing is often the very thing that had disappeared for Job. As he wraps up his lament, Job spends the remainder of chapter 29 mourning the loss of one final pillar of his prime. And of all the pillars, this one was by far the most public.

In the ancient world, official business was often conducted at the city gates. It was the equivalent of our modern-day main street or business district. As Job approached these gates and took his "seat in the square," the picture he paints of his experience is striking:

> The young men saw me and hid themselves, And the old men arose and stood. The princes stopped talking and put their hands on their mouths; the voice of the nobles was hushed, and their tongue stuck to their palate . . . To me they listened and waited, and kept silent for my counsel. After my words they did not speak again, and my speech dropped on them. They waited for me as for the rain, and opened their mouth as for the spring rain.[2]

Job's position was one of prominence. There was no class of person who did not demonstrate deference to him. Young men would make themselves invisible in his presence. The elders of the community would force their arthritic knees to stand as a show of respect. The nobility would relinquish their birthright to speak so that Job's weighty words could be heard by all. And once he spoke, no one would offer anything in the way of refutation. His was always the last word. Like dry ground eager to soak up a spring rain, so were Job's contemporaries as they waited to hear his counsel.

If I were to sum up the experience Job describes in this passage with one word it would be this: honor. For Job, the disappearance of honor was the insult Satan had decided to add to the injury of a

2. Job 29:8–10, 21–23.

(seemingly) lost friendship with God, the death of his children, and material bankruptcy. And the loss of honor was no small slight. In chapter 29, Job employs a mere six verses to bring us to this point. But he devotes the rest of the chapter, nineteen verses in all, to unpack in detail the important place honor held in the prime of his days.

Why so much focus on honor? We'll get into that as we unpack this chapter. But let me start by saying I think there is a hint of prophecy in this passage of Job. Honor is a cultural diagnostic of sorts. Job knew firsthand that where honor exists, God's children flourish. When honor erodes, despair soon follows. Job's personal anguish serves as a harbinger of what's to come when we neglect to honor God and our fellow man. Take another look at the quoted passage above and answer the following questions:

1. Have you ever experienced honor to the degree Job did in these verses?

2. When was the last time you sought to bestow honor to the extent Job's contemporaries did?

If we're honest with ourselves, the answers to these questions are alarming. If the experience of honor is starting to feel foreign to you, it's because it too often is.

THE DECLINE OF HONOR

Let me share an observation with you. I was born in January 1981. For the first week of my life, President Carter was the Commander-in-Chief. But my first memories of the presidency begin with President Reagan. As a child of the eighties I noticed that for the bulk of my childhood, and even into my teen years, the President always seemed to have two names. Whether he was being referred to by citizens, politicians, or pundits, he was nearly always called by his first name (in this case, his title: President), followed by his last name (insert surname here). Referring to the President by his title was a small, yet important way of honoring the office, if not the man. And if memory serves, nearly everyone did it. At least the first time they mentioned him in a given conversation.

But something happened as I approached adolescence and progressed into young adulthood. The President lost his first name. Like pop stars, Presidents started going by singular monikers. The President Reagan and President Bush (41) of my youth had been replaced by Bush (43), Obama, and Trump in the political parlance of my adulthood. Rarely does anyone seem to refer to the President by his title anymore unless it's by a member of his own party or by a sympathetic news outlet. And even then, the usage is inconsistent at best.

Neglecting to honor the title of office holders has not been limited to the political arena. I'm also struck by how casual we've become when referring to the leaders of our churches. There was a time when none of us would dream of referring to our ministers as anything other than "Pastor" or "Reverend." Yet today, even when performing sacraments, it's not unusual to hear a church leader referred to simply as "Bill" or "Mike."

And not to belabor the point, but when was the last time you heard someone refer to their elder as "Sir" or "Ma'am"? Even generic, respectful pronouns like these have been largely jettisoned from our modern lexicon. Now, before I develop a reputation as a curmudgeon, let me just say that I am not a crusader for formality. Most who know me would say that I prefer a laidback, casual atmosphere most of the time, especially around those with whom I've built a rapport.

But the shift in the way we address others is a surface level symptom of a much deeper cultural abandonment of honor. Dr. Albert Mohler, president of Southern Baptist Theological Seminary, characterizes this abandonment well:

> We live in an age that increasingly sees honor as a problem to be overcome rather than a virtue to be achieved. Honor is like a piece of furniture we would never want the neighbors to see, an antique that is hidden in the basement. The sociologist Peter Berger once described honor, like chastity, as obsolete in modern secular cultures. "At best," he said, "honor and chastity are seen as ideological

leftovers in the consciousness of obsolete classes, such as military officers or ethnic grandmothers."[3]

The implications of an honor-less culture are legion. That's because honor serves as the bedrock of biblical ethics. The first commandment concerning our relations with our fellow man begins with the directive to honor our parents.[4] Why? In part, it's because without honor the rest of the Ten Commandments collapse like a house of cards:

- A failure to honor the sanctity of life leads to murder.
- A failure to honor marriage leads to adultery.
- A failure to honor ownership leads to theft.
- A failure to honor truth leads to deception.
- A failure to honor God's provision leads to covetousness.

Job's testimony is powerful because it underscores the important place honor must hold in our lives and in our culture. Like a lynchpin, honor helps ensure our ethical framework holds together. Without it, everything quickly falls apart.

THE IMPORTANCE OF HONOR

The Command to Honor

Honor wasn't just an important pillar of the prime of Job's life. It's an important pillar of the Christian faith. The fifth commandment is far from the only place where God commands us to bestow honor. Subjects deserving honor are scattered throughout the Bible. They include [commands to honor]:

God: "Now to the King eternal, immortal, invisible, the only God, be *honor* and glory forever and ever. Amen."[5]

---

3. Mohler, "Honor Lost Altogether?"
4. Exod 20:12.
5. 1 Tim 1:17, emphasis mine.

Our bodies: ". . . that each of you know how to possess his own vessel in sanctification and *honor*."[6]

The sabbath: ". . . call the sabbath a delight, the holy day of the Lord *honorable*, and *honor* it."[7]

Our elders: "You shall rise up before the grayheaded and *honor* the aged."[8]

Church elders: "The elders who rule well are to be considered worth of double *honor*."[9]

Marriage: "Marriage is to be held in *honor* among all."[10]

Wives: "You husbands, live with your wives . . . and show her *honor* . . ."[11]

Widows: "*Honor* widows who are widows indeed."[12]

Do-gooders: ". . . but glory and *honor* and peace to everyone who does good."[13]

Fellow believers: "Be devoted to one another in brotherly love; give preference to one another in *honor*."[14]

Everyone: "*Honor* all people . . ."[15]

Leaders: ". . . *honor* the king."[16]

God (again): "Worthy are you, our Lord and our God, to receive glory and *honor* and power . . ."[17]

---

6. 1 Thess 4:4, emphasis mine.

7. Isa 58:13, emphasis mine.

8. Lev 19:32, emphasis mine.

9. 1 Tim 5:17, emphasis mine.

10. Heb 13:4, emphasis mine.

11. 1 Pet 3:7, emphasis mine.

12. 1 Tim 5:3, emphasis mine.

13. Rom 2:10, emphasis mine.

14. Rom 12:10, emphasis mine.

15. 1 Pet 2:17a, emphasis mine.

16. 1 Pet 2:17b, emphasis mine.

17. Rev 4:11, emphasis mine.

The subject of honor permeates Scripture because the practice of honor should permeate the Christian life. The question of, "Whom can I honor today?" should be one every Christian prayerfully asks on a daily basis. God often uses repetition in his word to hammer home things that are important to him. When it comes to honor, he has pounded his point securely. The question is, will we hold fast?

The Blessings of Honor

If the repeated voice of Scripture isn't enough to spur us on toward honor, the benefits we derive from honoring others should be. An opportunity to please God with our obedience is more than enough reason to continuously seek to honor others. But God has been gracious enough to sweeten the deal with promises from his word should we follow through on his command. We've already covered that the concept of honor finds its root in the fifth commandment's directive to honor our parents. But let us not gloss over the amazing promise that is attached to our obedience:

> ". . . so that it may be well with you, and that you may live long on the earth."[18]

The measure of blessing and longevity we experience in life is directly related to our obedience in the area of honor. Is it any wonder that Job, a man whose prime of life was marked by honor at every turn, was also the most blessed man of his age? Isn't it interesting that after recounting the loss of his material blessings, Job immediately mentions the disappearance of honor from his life? Blessing and honor are intrinsically linked.

But we must be careful as we port this passage into our modern context. We live in a very materialistic society. It would be tempting to infer that obedience in the area of honor will lead directly to material or financial blessing. It's crucial that we don't put God in a box. Blessing comes in many forms. The promise "that it may be well with you" is worded in an open-ended manner. This is no

18. Eph 6:3.

accident, and we should be glad for that. God doesn't limit himself in the way he chooses to bless us. He provides the blessing we need, when we need it, in the form we need it. He may bless us with good health. He may bless us with loving relationships. He may bless us with spiritual insights. He may bless us with exciting opportunities. He may bless us with peace. He may bless us with reconciliation. He may bless us with an encouraging word.

The possibilities for blessing are boundless. But the promise remains. If we are faithful to provide the honor, God is faithful to provide the blessing.

The Power of Honor

If obedience to God's word and the promise of blessing weren't enough to sell you on the importance of honor, Scripture offers one final kicker. It comes straight from the life and ministry of Jesus. And the implications couldn't be bigger.

But first, let's provide a little background. In Matthew 13 we see Jesus returning to his hometown of Nazareth. Not to be confused with Bethlehem (where he was born), Nazareth is where Jesus spent the majority of his life after his family's return from Egypt and prior to the start of his public ministry. It's where he grew up. It's where he went to school. It's where he learned his father's trade of carpentry. The local synagogue is where he would've worshipped with his family.

But it wasn't exactly a happy homecoming. This "visit to Nazareth came about a year after the citizens of the town had attempted to murder Jesus (Luke 4:29)."[19] After calling them out (correctly) on the fact that they were more interested in the eloquence of his speech and the miracles he had performed than in the message of the gospel, they literally tried to throw him off a cliff. When you think about it, it's incredible that Jesus returned at all. But our Lord is a Lord who is longsuffering and gracious, even to his enemies. Matthew provides us the account of his return visit:

19. Thomas and Gundry, *Harmony of the Gospels*, 94.

> He came to His hometown and began teaching them in
> their synagogue, so that they were astonished, and said,
> "Where did this man get this wisdom and these miracu-
> lous powers? Is not this the carpenter's son? Is not His
> mother called Mary, and His brothers, James and Joseph
> and Simon and Judas? And His sisters, are they not all
> with us? Where then did this man get all these things?"
> And they took offense at Him. But Jesus said to them,
> "A prophet is not without honor except in his hometown
> and in his own household." And He did not do many
> miracles there because of their unbelief.[20]

The reception wasn't all that much warmer than his previous
visit. The locals were still impressed by his teaching. But instead
of letting the words sink into their hearts, they chose to train their
minds on what they *thought* they knew about Jesus. They simply
couldn't fathom that someone who had grown up alongside them,
been babysat by their sister, played with them after school, or fash-
ioned a table for their uncle could be so bold as to exercise authority
as the Chosen One of God. The old adage that "familiarity breeds
contempt" could not be a more apt description for the dynamic
unfolding in this passage.

And what was the result? Jesus did not do many miracles
there. The Gospel accounts describe Jesus performing miraculous
signs and wonders nearly everywhere he traveled across Judea,
Samaria, and Galilee. What was it about his hometown that made
him unwilling to demonstrate his power in the same way there?
Put simply: a lack of honor. Jesus said it himself, He was honored
everywhere he went *except* in his own hometown. Honor was the
missing link.

My great-grandfather was fond of saying, "talk is cheap, it
takes money to buy whiskey." If we lend the sentiment of his "Ne-
braska-ism" to this passage, we might say that a desire to hear God's
word and see him do miraculous things is cheap. It takes honor to
secure power in God's kingdom. Honor is the currency of kingdom
economy. With it, our faith can procure mighty things; without it,
our faith can procure little. Just ask the citizens of Nazareth.

20. Matt 13:54–58.

When it comes to our faith, the importance of honor cannot be overstated. Matthew's account is clear. A lack of honor does not merely reflect a lack of maturity. It reflects a lack of belief. A desire to honor God and his image bearers is woven into the very fabric of our faith. May we give the Spirit free reign when he approaches that faith with his needle and thread.

WHY DON'T WE SEEK HONOR?

All of this begs a question. If God commands that we honor him and our fellow man, if bestowing honor leads to blessing, and if honor is the key that unlocks the power of God's kingdom, then why don't we seek it more? Let me offer a few educated guesses.

We Settle

When it comes to honor, we too often settle for something less. As we've discussed thus far, honor is weighty. Honor is powerful. Honor is a pillar of the prime of life. Yet, when it comes to honor, we are tempted to accept its counterfeit instead: simply being noticed. Popularity is a poor substitute for honor, but it's what we too often shoot for. This may sound out of step in this day and age, but garnering "likes" on a social media platform is rarely akin to receiving honor. It's hard to truly honor someone with a finger tap on a screen.

Honor requires deference. Honor requires that we elevate the subject of our esteem. Honor requires intentionality. Honor often requires a personal touch. Providing honor is rarely as simple as the click of a button or the tap of a screen, but the effects are much more impactful, and not nearly as fleeting.

We Wait

Scripture tells us it's more blessed to give than to receive.[21] And although this statement is used in the context of material giving,

---

21. Acts 20:35.

the same could be said of honor. As we've covered already, blessing awaits those who give honor to whom it is due. However, many of us forego this blessing by waiting to provide honor until it has first been provided to us. The mindset of "Why should I honor them? They've never so much as complimented me" is an easy one to adopt. But it doesn't lead us where we need to go. I'm preaching to myself most of all when I exhort all of us to boldly be the first to honor others in our relationships.

We Add Conditions

Remember all of those commands to honor from Scripture listed earlier? One of the reasons we fail to obey them is because we add (seemingly) small conditions to them. These little amendments usually begin with "as long as" and often sound something like this:

- I'll honor God, *as long as* I don't feel like he's withholding something from me.
- I'll honor my body, *as long as* it feels good.
- I'll honor the sabbath, *as long as* I'm not too busy that week.
- I'll honor my elders, *as long as* I appreciate their legacy.
- I'll honor my church's elders, *as long as* I agree with the way they're running things.
- I'll honor marriage, *as long as* it doesn't get too tough.
- I'll honor my wife, *as long as* she's meeting my expectations.
- I'll honor widows, *as long as* it's convenient for me.
- I'll honor those who do good, *as long as* it doesn't make me feel guilty.
- I'll honor fellow believers, *as long as* I never see them sin.
- I'll honor everyone, *as long as* they don't annoy me.
- I'll honor our leaders, *as long as* I voted for them.

If you're anything like me, too many of these statements sound familiar. One of the most challenging things in the Christian faith is to honor those whom you deem to not be worthy of it. Or to honor others when it's far easier to honor ourselves and our own desires. Honoring unconditionally is excruciatingly difficult. But it's exactly what God's word calls us to do. Failing to do so not only robs God of the obedience he is due; it robs us of living life in our prime.

We Value the Wrong Things

While there is no question that honor is in decline, it has not disappeared. We tend to honor what we value. And long as there are things we hold dear, there will be things upon which we bestow honor. But often that honor is misplaced. Why? Because we value the wrong things.

Let me use an example from the professional ranks. Perhaps the most basic form of honor in the workplace comes in the form of a job offer. In theory, an organization will honor the candidate whose experience, credentials, and interview responses best align with what the organization declares to value in the role (as published in the job posting) with an offer of employment. In practice, this is often not the case.

A candidate may submit a resumé that checks all the boxes. They may reference prior projects in a phone screening that demonstrate they'd be ideally suited to tackle this sort of work. They may provide answers in a behavioral interview that indicate they could adeptly navigate the hierarchy of the organization.

But when the hiring committee convenes to discuss the candidate's qualifications, something strange happens. Heretofore unmentioned qualities that the candidate is lacking come to light:

- "I know he has his bachelor's, *but* he didn't get it from Tech."
- "She's had tremendous success elsewhere, *but* she doesn't look like the rest of our sales team."
- "This isn't a leadership role, *but* I really wish he had some management experience."
- "She's a thought leader in her field, *but* she's never worked in higher ed before."

One by one, the qualities the hiring committee truly values begin to surface. And they start to supplant the qualities that were communicated to the candidate (and even some of the hiring committee) in the job posting and in prior interviews. Unfortunately, this too often leads to organizations making poor hiring decisions. This is because they choose to honor what they value instead of choosing to honor what they *should* value. And what's more unfortunate is that these unpublished and misplaced values cost the ideal candidate the honor of a job that should've been theirs.

When organizations value the wrong things, they miss out on the best talent. When we value the wrong things, we miss out on honor. We end up honoring things that aren't truly deserving of honor, and we fail to provide honor where honor is due. As a result, we forfeit our "seat in the square," and with it an important pillar of the prime of life. As humans, we will never fail to honor what we value. As Christians, we must never stop asking, "Am I honoring what *God* values?"

HOW CAN WE RESURRECT HONOR?

I've painted a pretty bleak picture thus far in this chapter. If honor is in decline, or at the very least misplaced, how can it be restored? Put simply, by living honorably. And in Job we are provided a template for honorable living. Remember back in Job 1 when God asked Satan to consider the character of his servant?

> . . . For there is no one like him on the earth, a blameless and upright man, fearing God and turning away from evil.[22]

By way of a crude paraphrase we might assert that God is describing Job as a man who values what God values, and honors what God honors. We can say this because of the way Job lived his life. In Job 29 we are given a mini-autobiography in which Job recounts the way he spent his time, energy, and resources. Remember, for Job, the world was his oyster. As the greatest man of the East, he had the means to live a life of luxury that would've rivaled Solomon's.

But instead, he chose to live a life of honor. It was a life that foreshadowed the sort of life Jesus would come to earth to live hundreds of years later. Remember in chapter 1 when I said that one of

22. Job 1:8.

our primary reasons for studying Job is that he points us to Christ? The verses that follow are where much of that pointing takes place. I've broken them out by the subject of Job's focus and provided a side-by-side reference to another passage, either from a Gospel account of Christ's life, or from another passage alluding to Christ:

The Poor and The Orphan

Job	Christ
For when the ear heard, it called me blessed, And when the eye saw, it gave witness of me, Because I delivered the poor who cried for help, And the orphan who had no helper. —Job 29:11–12	. . . The unfortunate commits himself to You; You have been the helper of the orphan. —Ps 10:14

The Perishing and The Widow

Job	Christ
The blessing of the one ready to perish came upon me, And I made the widow's heart sing for joy. —Job 29:13	Soon afterwards He went to a city called Nain; and His disciples were going along with Him, accompanied by a large crowd. Now as He approached the gate of the city, a dead man was being carried out, the only son of his mother, and she was a widow; and a sizeable crowd from the city was with her. When the Lord saw her, He felt compassion for her, and said to her, "Do not weep." And He came up and touched the coffin; and the bearers came to a halt. And He said, "Young man, I say to you, arise!" The dead man sat up and began to speak. And Jesus gave him back to his mother. —Luke 7:11–15

Righteousness and Justice

Job	Christ
I put on righteousness, and it clothed me; My justice was like a robe and a turban. —Job 29:14	as it is written, "He scattered abroad, He gave to the poor, His righteousness endures forever." —2 Cor 9:9 Behold, my servant whom I have chosen; my beloved in whom my soul is well-pleased; I will put my spirit upon him, and he shall proclaim justice to the Gentiles. —Matt 12:18

The Blind and The Lame

Job	Christ
I was eyes to the blind and feet to the lame. —Job 29:15	Jesus answered and said to them, "Go and report to John what you hear and see: the blind receive sight and the lame walk . . ." —Matt 11:4–5

Father to The Needy

Job	Christ
I was a father to the needy . . . —Job 29:16a	". . . because of the groaning of the needy, Now I will arise," says the LORD; "I will set him in the safety for which he longs." —Ps 12:5

Investigator

Job	Christ
. . . And I investigated the case which I did not know. —Job 29:16b	The scribes and the Pharisees brought a woman caught in adultery, and having set her in the center of the court, they said to Him, "Teacher, this woman has been caught in adultery, in the very act. Now in the Law Moses commanded us to stone such women; what then do You say?" They were saying this, testing Him, so that they might have grounds for accusing Him. But Jesus stooped down and with His finger wrote on the ground. But when they persisted in asking Him, He straightened up, and said to them, "He who is without sin among you, let him be the first to throw a stone at her." Again He stooped down and wrote on the ground. When they heard it, they began to go out one by one, beginning with the older ones, and He was left alone, and the woman, where she was, in the center of the court. Straightening up, Jesus said to her, "Woman, where are they? Did no one condemn you?" She said, "No one, Lord." And Jesus said, "I do not condemn you, either. Go. From now on sin no more." —John 8:3–11

Breaking the Jaws of the Wicked

Job	David (another type of Christ)
I broke the jaws of the wicked And snatched the prey from his teeth. —Job 29:17	But David said to Saul, "Your servant was tending his father's sheep. When a lion or a bear came and took a lamb from the flock, I went out after him and attacked him, and rescued it from his mouth; and when he rose up against me, I seized him by his beard and struck him and killed him. Your servant has killed both the lion and the bear; and this uncircumcised Philistine will be like one of them, since he has taunted the armies of the living God." And David said, "The LORD who delivered me from the paw of the lion and from the paw of the bear, He will deliver me from the hand of this Philistine." And Saul said to David, "Go, and may the LORD be with you." —1 Sam 17:34–37

Chief, King, Comforter

Job	Christ
I chose a way for them and sat as chief, And dwelt as a king among the troops, As one who comforted the mourners. —Job 29:25	For a child will be born to us, a son will be given to us; And the government will rest on His shoulders; And His name will be called Wonderful Counselor, Mighty God, Eternal Father, Prince of Peace. —Isa 9:6

The parallels are striking. Job points us to Christ because his values were so very Christ-like. The result was not a perfect life; only Jesus can claim that. But Job did lead a life of honor. He did so in multiple ways.

The Honor of Wealth Well Spent

First, Job honored the dignity of his fellow man, and in turn, the God whose image he bears. Job did not spend his time, energy, and resources on the sort of people you would expect him to. Neither did Jesus. As the greatest man of the East, one would expect Job to spend the majority of his time rubbing shoulders with the elite of ancient Uz. I like to picture Job standing on the red carpet of whatever the ancient Uzzian equivalent of the Oscars was. His immense wealth would've granted him access to this or any other glamorous event taking place in his day. But Job did not use his wealth to secure access for himself. He used it to provide security to the least of those around him. The poor, the orphan, the perishing, the widow, the blind, the lame, and the needy held a special place in Job's heart and in his estate. They still hold a special place in God's heart and in his kingdom.

Job understood what too few of us who are wealthy fully grasp.[23] First, that the wealth we've been entrusted with is truly not our own. The church father, Basil of Caesarea, put it bluntly when he said, "A man who has two coats or two pairs of shoes when his neighbor has none has his neighbor's coat and shoes."[24] Job knew that his wealth was not provided merely for his own personal comfort or enjoyment; it was provided to supply those in need.

Second, Job realized that the stewardship of material blessing is a critical component embedded in the process of sanctification. John Wimber, founder of the Vineyard Church movement, asserted this was foundational to our faith when he said, "We need the poor to work out our own salvation, and the poor need us."[25] Wealth is something that is rarely held well. Most of us would probably do well to echo the prayer of Agur, who feared that pride would accompany riches and so asked God to moderate his finances.[26]

23. Odds are if you had the disposable income to buy this book, and the disposable time to read it at your leisure, then yes, you qualify as being wealthy.
24. as cited in Wimber, *The Way In*, 65.
25. Wimber, *The Way In*, 57.
26. Prov 30:7–9.

But for those of us who find ourselves stewarding a surplus, we should ask ourselves, "where is God's heart?" Wherever that is, our surplus should follow. I'm not saying that we should never enjoy the blessings of luxury from time to time. After all, Job and his family were no strangers to opulence. Odds are, the frequent parties thrown by his sons were supplied either directly from Job's immense holdings, or indirectly via some early form of inheritance. In and of itself, enjoying these material blessings is not a bad thing. But Job 29 tells us where Job's heart was when it came to money, as well as the purpose of money in the economy of God's kingdom.

The Honor of Influence Well Wielded

Another way in which Job lived out his life of honor was by combating the injustices and unrighteousness inherent in the fallen world around him. By doing so, he honored the God who is completely just, completely righteous, and will one day claim complete victory in a new heaven and new earth.[27] Job's standing as the greatest man of the East was not merely a function of his immense wealth, it was also a function of his immense influence. Job possessed both, and more importantly, wielded both well.

For Job, his "seat in the square" afforded him a powerful voice in civic matters. With this power came a great deal of freedom. Pulitzer prize-winning biographer, Robert Caro, said of power that "it always reveals what you wanted to do all along. . . . I think that what's always true is that power reveals, because when you have enough power to do whatever you want to do, then people see what you wanted to do."[28] I think the difference between great men of power and great men of honor is that the former use their power as a means of doing what they want, while the latter use their power as a means of doing what they ought. Job was certainly one of the latter.

Scripture tells us nothing about what Job wanted or desired to do with his influence. But Job 29 tells us plenty about what he ought to have done, and ultimately did do with it. Job didn't just

27. Rev 21:1–5.
28. Caro, "Lyndon B. Johnson," 136.

use his influence to secure the rights and interests of himself and his family. He used his influence to secure the rights and interests of those who couldn't secure it for themselves. Job's civic duty went beyond charity. It extended to the active defense of the defenseless. As a magistrate, he would investigate and dismiss the cases of those wrongly accused. As a justice of the peace, he would rescue those easily preyed on by the seedier elements of society. In doing so, he defended the honor of his fellow man, as well as his own.

The Honor of Empathetic Leadership

In Job 29:25 we see Job assuming the mantle of leadership. He describes himself as making decisions on behalf of the people, sitting as chief, and dwelling as a king would. These descriptions are certainly in keeping with most notions of leadership. But he ends the verse with a statement that almost seems out of place. In the same breath he mentions that he was "one who comforted mourners." How does comforting mourners qualify as a tenet of leadership? What does empathy have to do with honor? In a word: everything.

Let me see if I can illustrate this using a modern picture of leadership. As an American, my mind automatically drifts toward the presidency when I think of leadership. The parallels are quite clear when you start to enumerate the various job duties of the chief executive. The President certainly makes decisions on behalf of the people. In fact, one could argue the job is primarily an onslaught of never-ending decisions to be made. Which department should get more funding? Which diplomat should be the next ambassador to nation X? Who should be the next nominee to the Supreme Court? We could go on and on. The President also certainly sits as Commander-in-Chief of our armed forces as stipulated in Article II of the U.S. Constitution. And the President dwells as a king would in the closest thing America has to a royal palace, the White House.

But the President has another job duty that is not specifically spelled out in the Constitution or even talked about all that often in the news. When the nation is facing a tragedy, the President often takes on the role of "Comforter-in-Chief." We expect our presidents to bravely lead us in times of war, deftly navigate the politics of Capitol Hill in order to advance their political agenda and represent the cause of freedom abroad. But when a crisis hits, we also expect them to demonstrate empathy toward their fellow citizens. Presidents hop on planes to visit sites of natural disasters, lay wreaths at historic battlefields, and make sympathy calls to the families of fallen soldiers because most of them realize that empathy is a critical component of leadership. It's also a hallmark of a life lived with honor.

Sadly, with a decline in honor comes a decline in empathy. And the results of this decline aren't pretty. The tribalism that characterizes our modern society is owed in large part to a cultural lack of empathy. It's easy to demonize "them" if we've never considered their worldview or taken the time to investigate and attempt to understand the experiences that helped shape it. It's certainly more fun for leaders to make decisions, sit as chief, or dwell as king, but if they lack empathy, they will soon find that they are leading only factions and not the whole of the people they were meant to lead. Leadership requires more than one's head. It also requires one's heart.

Job's "seat in the square" was reserved for him, not just because he made prudent decisions on behalf of the people and looked the part of a leader, but because he took the time to love those he led when they were hurting. By doing so he honored their humanity as well as the God whose image they bore. By doing so, he led his people with honor. And by doing so, he points us to a Savior who aches as we ache[29] when faced with the tragedies of life.

Matthew Henry, the famous Bible commentator, said of this aspect of Job's character, "It is a pleasure to a good man, and should be so to a great man, to give those occasion to rejoice that are most acquainted with grief."[30] As his people's "Comforter-in-Chief," Job derived pleasure from bringing comfort to those who needed it. As a result, his contemporaries (and God) esteemed him not just as a good man, but as a great man. I pray that each of us would find the pleasure in empathy that Job found. The world is in desperate need of it.

29. John 11:35.
30. Henry, *Commentary*.

In summing up Job's life of honor, I will once more defer to Henry:

> What a great deal of good he did in his place. He was very serviceable to his country with the power he had; and here we shall see what it was which Job valued himself by in the day of his prosperity. It is natural to men to have some value for themselves, and we may judge something of our own character by observing what that is upon which we value ourselves. Job valued himself, not by the honour of his family, the great estate he had, his large income, his full table, the many servants he had at his command, the ensigns of his dignity, his equipage and retinue, the splendid entertainments he gave, and the court that was made to him, but by his usefulness.[31]

Honor can be traced directly to one's values. And Job valued himself by his usefulness. He understood what too few of us grasp too late in life. That our wealth, resources, time, energy, and influence are best spent not on ourselves, but on those God has put in our path. What a "great deal of good" we can do in our place if we seek a life of honor! And what a great deal of honor we can bestow upon our Lord in the process.

31. Henry, *Commentary.*

Epilogue

And Job died an old man and full of days.

—JOB 42:17

The bulk of this book has been dedicated to exploring the prime of life of Job, the greatest man of his day by almost any definition. But the text is delivered by way of remembrance. As Job laments the loss of his prime, we can't forget that he is speaking to us from a place of brokenness that most of us could never comprehend. So, what ever happened to Job? Did he finally succumb to Satan's torment? Did he linger on in destitution for the rest of his life? Did God take mercy on him and end his life and suffering? Did he ever find restoration? For the answer we must skip ahead to the final chapter of Job's story:

> The LORD restored the fortunes of Job when he prayed for his friends, and the LORD increased all that Job had twofold. Then all his brothers and all his sisters and all who had known him before came to him, and they ate bread with him in his house; and they consoled him and comforted him for all the adversities that the LORD had brought on him. And each one gave him one piece of money, and each a ring of gold. The LORD blessed the latter days of Job more than his beginning; and he had 14,000 sheep and 6,000 camels and 1,000 yoke of oxen and 1,000 female donkeys. He had seven sons and three daughters. He named the first Jemimah, and the second

Keziah, and the third Keren-happuch. In all the land no women were found so fair as Job's daughters; and their father gave them inheritance among their brothers. After this, Job lived 140 years, and saw his sons and his grandsons, four generations. And Job died, an old man and full of days.[1]

You will be hard pressed to find a greater reversal of fortune anywhere in Scripture. Job experienced what few others have . . . a second prime of life. And the striking thing is that all four pillars of his first prime were stood back up in his second, only twice as tall. Taking them in reverse order, we see that Job got his honor back. His brothers, sisters, and all his acquaintances sought to be in his presence. They enjoyed the intimacy of a shared meal with him. And they each gifted him a piece of money and a ring of gold. Not because he was in material need, but as tokens signifying the rightful return of Job to his "seat in the square."

The almost unfathomable material wealth of Job was not only restored but doubled. Imagine the headlines if Warren Buffett, Bill Gates, or Jeff Bezos had their fortunes doubled. That's exactly what happened to Job! His seven thousand original sheep were replaced with fourteen thousand new ones. His three thousand lost camels replaced with six thousand more. Twice the number of yokes would've been necessary to employ his one thousand new oxen. The doubling continued with his female donkeys.[2] For a man who understood the true purpose of wealth, he was given twice the fortune to steward during his second prime.

Job was also given a second chance to enjoy the presence of children. Having lost ten children in a fashion few would recover from, God saw fit to bless Job with ten more. Again, seven sons and three daughters graced his household, and each would receive a share of his now doubled inheritance.

Lastly, though I would argue that it never truly went away, Job was allowed to once again feel the thing he desired most . . . the friendship of God. By asking Job to intercede in prayer on behalf of

---

1. Job 42:10–17.
2. Still no word on the male donkeys. Am I the only one bothered by that?

his friends, God made it clear to Job that the lines of communication with him were open once again. Not only that, but intercession assumes a bold and confident access reserved only for the friends of God.[3] And Job would enjoy this friendship uninterrupted for the remaining 140 years of his life.

And so it was that Job would enjoy a second prime of life, twice as blessed as his first. The book of Job has what my wife and I refer to as a "Disney ending," in that everything works out nice and neat and happy in the end. But as we look to apply the lessons found in Job to our own lives, a disconnect can quickly emerge. Like Job, many of us have experienced a season we would describe as the prime of our life. And many of us can relate to having lost it. But not all of us can relate to having it restored. In fact, many of us are still waiting for our next "ship to come in."

Take as an example the events of my own life. At the time of my writing this, it's been three-and-a-half years since that no good, very bad February day I recounted in the Prologue. A lot has happened since then. My father-in-law passed away in August of that year. The last two weeks of his life were two of the most trying of mine. My wife's epilepsy was finally brought under control by a new drug. And while we are incredibly grateful for the respite in her health, in the back of our minds we worry about the drug's long-term side effects. My wife and I are still zombies. Our kids bring us immense joy, but they have never brought us anything resembling immense rest. We still live in the same community, where I've even managed to make a couple of friends over the last few years. But I wouldn't exactly describe my environment as fertile with fellowship.

Life has been what it so often is, a mixed bag. What it's not been is my prime. When I read about the restoration of Job, I praise God for the testimony of a righteous man who received the redemption he deserved. But I am left with a lingering question. How am I to reconcile the experience of Job with my own? As I make my way through life, I still encounter hurts and hang-ups along the way. And if I'm perfectly honest, the "momentary, light afflictions" that Paul describes rarely feel momentary or light as I experience

3. Eph 3:12.

them.[4] Is the "Disney ending" found in Job just a tease? Is it the testimony of an ancient patriarch to whom I can't relate? The answer to these questions, I think, is found in Job's daughters.

. . . no women were found so fair . . .

Of Job's twenty children, none are mentioned by name, except his second set of daughters. Job makes it a point to mention each of the three by their given name. He does so because names are important. And in the Bible names nearly always carry with them a meaning deeper than the way they sound rolling off the tongue. In this case, each of Job's daughters bears a name signifying an aspect of his restoration.

If we break out a lexicon, we see that the first daughter's name, Jemimah, means "day" or "day by day."[5] This is in sharp contrast to the "dark night of the soul" her father had emerged from.[6] The second daughter's name, Keziah, means "cassia," a tree whose stem and bark produce a cinnamon-like fragrance used in a variety of spice mixtures. This is in contrast with the stench that must have emanated from Job's open wounds that he nursed in vain during Satan's attack on his health. The third daughter's name, Keren-happuch, means "horn of antimony." Antimony was a mineral used to make cosmetics, specifically an ancient form of eye shadow. This beautification of the eyes stands in sharp contrast with the tear-stained eyes of Job as he lamented his many misfortunes.

---

4. 2 Cor 4:17a.

5. Brown et al., *NAS Hebrew Lexicon.*

6. As soon as I finish writing this, I'm bumping the church history classic with this title by St. John of the Cross to the top of my reading list.

The names of Job's daughters point beautifully to the restoration of his prime. But that's not the only thing they point to. As we hold up the meaning of their names to the pages of Scripture, we see that they describe something else as well:

Jemimah	The New Jerusalem
"day" "day by day"	In the daytime (for there will be no night there) its gates will never be closed. —Rev 21:25 And there will no longer be any night; and they will not have need of the light of a lamp nor the light of the sun, because the Lord God will illumine them; and they will reign forever and ever. —Rev 22:5

Keziah	Jesus
"cassia" (fragrant)	You have loved righteousness and hated wickedness; Therefore God, Your God, has anointed You With the oil of joy above Your fellows. All Your garments are fragrant with myrrh and aloes and cassia . . . —Ps 45:7–8

Keren-happuch	The New Jerusalem
"horn of antimony" (beautiful eyes)	and He will wipe away every tear from their eyes; and there will no longer be any death; there will no longer be any mourning, or crying, or pain; the first things have passed away. —Rev 21:4

It turns out that Job's daughters don't just paint a picture of their father's life. They paint a picture of the eternal life our Heavenly Father has in store for those who believe. A life where darkness is banished, where the fragrance of our Lord's righteousness will meet us at every turn, and where tears, death, mourning, crying, and pain will be a distant memory.

When Scripture tells us that "in all the land no women were found so fair as Job's daughters," it's not merely describing the physical attributes or character traits of Job's three lovely daughters. It's also not simply alluding to the "fairness" of Job's life after he had been restored. It's pointing us to the incomparable beauty of an eternity spent with Christ.

You see, Job holds incredible lessons for how to live a life pleasing to God here on Earth. But perhaps the greatest lesson we can learn from Job is this: the true prime of our days is not to be found in this life; it's to be found in the next. And for those who believe, the weight of glory we shall bear will be beyond compare.[7]

7. 2 Cor 4:17b.

A Prayer for Your Prime

I hope this book has in some small way been a blessing, an encouragement, or a revelation to you. I would be remiss if I let you leave this final page without first offering a prayer for your own prime:

> Father God, I pray for the reader of this book.
> I pray that they would have the opportunity to taste, if only for a little while, what it's like to live life in its prime.
> I pray that they would accept and enjoy the incredible gift of friendship you offer.
> I pray that they would devote their time and talents to the consecration of those you give them the privilege of parenting.
> I pray that you would bless them with the material resources they need to be a blessing to others.
> I pray that they would live lives of honor.
> And I pray that they would wait expectantly for the "prime of life" that is an eternity spent with you.
> Amen.

Bibliography

Bhattacharya, Kunal. "Sex Differences in Social Focus Across the Life Cycle in Humans." *Royal Society Open Science* 3 (April 2016). https://www.ncbi.nlm.nih.gov/pmc/articles/PMC4852646/.

Bichell, Rae Ellen. "Average Age of First-Time Moms Keeps Climbing In The U.S." *National Public Radio*, January 14, 2016. https://www.npr.org/sections/health-shots/2016/01/14/462816458/average-age-of-first-time-moms-keeps-climbing-in-the-u-s.

Blount, Roy Jr. "Making Sense of Robert E. Lee." *Smithsonian Magazine*, July 2003. https://www.smithsonianmag.com/history/making-sense-of-robert-e-lee-85017563/#J2gjD7fsw4ozjBxT.99.

Brown, Driver, et al. *The NAS Old Testament Hebrew Lexicon*. Camarillo, CA: Salem Media Group, 2019. https://www.biblestudytools.com/lexicons/hebrew/nas/.

Caro, Robert. "Lyndon B. Johnson." In *The Presidents: Noted Historians Rank America's Best—and Worst—Chief Executives*, edited by Brian Swain et al., 126–138. New York: Public Affairs, 2019.

Gill, John. *John Gill's Exposition of the Bible*. Camarillo, CA: Salem Media Group, 2019. https://www.biblestudytools.com/commentaries/gills-exposition-of-the-bible/.

Henry, Matthew. *Matthew Henry Commentary on the Whole Bible (Complete)*. Camarillo, CA: Salem Media Group, 2019. https://www.biblestudytools.com/commentaries/matthew-henry-complete/.

Lee, Peter Y. "The Surprising Source of Joy: A Biblical Foundation for Christ-Centered Suffering." *Reformed Faith & Practice* 3 (Summer 2018).

Lewis, C. S. *The Four Loves*. New York: Harcourt, 1960.

Mohler, Albert. "What If Honor Is Lost Altogether?" *TableTalk Magazine*, February 2019. https://tabletalkmagazine.com/article/2019/02/honor-lost-altogether/.

Perritt, John. *Your Days Are Numbered: A Closer Look At How We Spend Our Time & The Eternity Before Us*. Geanies House, UK: Christian Focus, 2016.

Pew Research Center. *Modern Parenthood*. March 14, 2013. https://www. pewsocialtrends.org/2013/03/14/chapter-5-americans-time-at-paid-work-housework-child-care-1965-to-2011/.

Robson, David, "What's the Prime of Your Life?" *BBC*, May 25, 2015. http:// www.bbc.com/future/story/20150525-whats-the-prime-of-your-life.

"The Secret of My Success (1987 film)." Wikipedia. 2019. https://en.wikipedia. org/wiki/The_Secret_of_My_Success_(1987_film). Last modified 16 September 2019.

Sproul, R. C. "TULIP and Reformed Theology: Preservation of the Saints." Ligonier Ministries. April 22, 2017. https://www.ligonier.org/blog/tulip-and-reformed-theology-perseverance-saints/.

State of the American Workplace. Omaha, NE: Gallup, 2017.

Teresa of Avila, St. *The Collected Works of Saint Teresa of Avila*. Vol. 1. Translated by Kieran Kavanaugh, OCD, and Otilio Rodriguez, OCD. Washington, DC: Institute of Carmelite Studies, 1976.

Thomas, Robert L. and Stanley N. Gundry. *A Harmony of the Gospels: New American Standard Version*. New York: HarperOne, 1978.

van Selms, A. *Job: A Practical Commentary*. Grand Rapids, MI: Eerdmans, 1985.

Warren, Rick. *The Purpose Driven Life*. Grand Rapids, MI: Zondervan, 2002.

Wimber, John. *The Way In is the Way On: John Wimber's Teachings and Writings on Life in Christ*. Boise, ID: Ampelon, 2006.